Cyndi Dale's insight into energy healing has
the power to transform the universe.

—Dr. Scott Peck and Shannon Peck,
founders of the Love Center and
the authors of *The Love You Deserve*

Cyndi Dale has a gift for showing people how to transform
spiritual philosophies into practical, everyday processes. Her
wonderful books teach us how to heal our minds, bodies,
and souls, and ultimately create the life we desire.

—Tina Johnson,
founder and producer of *Mind, Body & Spirit*
television and radio series

Kundenjtut

About the Author

Cyndi Dale is internationally recognized as an authority on subtle energy anatomy. She is the author of several books on energy healing, including the original and revised *New Chakra Healing* (now called *The Complete Book of Chakra Healing*), which has been published in more than ten languages, and six other best-selling books on the topic, including *Advanced Chakra Healing, Illuminating the Afterlife,* and *The Subtle Body*. Through her company, Essential Energy, she provides intuitive assessments and life-issues healing for thousands of clients a year, seeking always to uplift and inspire others toward their true purposes and personalities. Her enthusiasm and care ignite all who attend her workshops, training sessions, and college classes, which are offered around the world.

Cyndi has studied cross-cultural healing and energy systems and has led instructional classes in many countries, including Peru, Costa Rica, Venezuela, Japan, Belize, Mexico, Morocco, Russia, and across Europe, as well as among the Lakota people and the Hawaiian kahunas. She currently lives in Minneapolis, Minnesota, with her two sons and (at last count) five pets.

More information about Cyndi's classes and products is available at www.cyndidale.com.

CYNDI DALE

Kundalini

Divine Energy
✳
Divine Life

Llewellyn Publications
WOODBURY, MINNESOTA

FIRST EDITION
Third Printing, 2013

Book design by Rebecca Zins
Cover design by Ellen Lawson
Cover image ©iStockphoto.com/chuwy
Interior illustrations by Llewellyn Art Department

Llewellyn is a registered trademark of Llewellyn Worldwide Ltd.

Library of Congress Cataloging-in-Publication Data
Dale, Cyndi.
 Kundalini : divine energy, divine life / Cyndi Dale.—1st ed.
   p. cm
 Includes bibliographical references and index.
 ISBN 978-0-7387-2588-8
 1. Kundalini. I. Title.
 BL1238.56.K86D35 2011
 204'.36—dc22
                                                    2010042495

Llewellyn Publications
A Division of Llewellyn Worldwide Ltd.
2143 Wooddale Drive
Woodbury, MN 55125-2989
www.llewellyn.com

Printed in the United States of America

Those who danced were thought to be quite insane by those who could not hear the music.

—Angela Monet

contents

Part II

Living with the Serpent: Kundalini in the Divine Life

Kundalini:
The Secret Doorway

Imagine that a door opens—a door that you didn't even know existed. A light beams from the other side, and you gasp. What's this light? Where does it come from? What are you supposed to do with it?

You aren't quite sure, but you sense immediate changes in your body. Is this light the secret to instant dieting, extra pocket change, hearts that beat together in rhythm? And is that a hint at a better sex life that you sense? You blush. Besides the desire to celebrate, to participate in the gala of life, you also perceive another mounting urgency, one you could only label as spiritual. The only way to say it is this: you feel called. You feel summoned by a sacred and watching power, one that knows your true soul. There is something important you are here on this planet to do, and this light will help you discover and accomplish it.

You glance around, not quite sure you want anyone noticing the transformational effects, especially those "kick up your heels" sensations. How are you going to explain these alterations to your friends and relatives, much less to yourself? In your search for an answer, you finally look at the door itself. Yes, there's a sign on it: KUNDALINI.

Whatever this is, you want more of it.

Everyone does—and has—since time began. Who wouldn't want to participate in the secret to longevity, health, wisdom, and, yes, sexual fulfillment? Whether you've already flung aside the gateway to kundalini or are simply standing at its entryway, you are ushering in a light, an energy, a divinely inspired and ancient power that has been center stage in spiritual communities throughout the history of the word.

Kundalini has long been known as a divine force and the key to enlightenment, as well as the secret power of bodily pleasures and joy. The best part is that you don't have to climb the stairway to heaven to find the entrance. To embrace its power, you don't need to follow a certain set of scriptures or wait until death do you part. You've only to search inside of yourself, and its wild, divine light becomes clearer. You've only to invite this "energy from the gods" forth to emblazon your own life force.

If you were able to fully draw on your kundalini, the life force that lies within, what might you do? Well, you could lasso the stars and pull them to earth, plant your dreams in the soil and grow love, laugh into the wind, and heal the world. You could write your name in the water, author your life, and sing with the Divine.

At some level, kundalini has already been accomplishing all this and more for you. You've already been exercising its enchantment to become the great person you are. As mysterious as its name and as magical as its origin, kundalini has been pulsing in your body since you were conceived, performing tasks as basic as igniting the electricity in your cells and as elusive as attracting others to you. Kundalini is a god energy, and as such, it nourishes your uniqueness and upholds your sacred vocation. Since it originates from the Divine Source, it also interconnects you with all living beings, as well as with the Divine itself. Because of these connections, to tap into your kundalini is to open the channel to your intuition, to begin to hear the messages in the wind, to receive revelations colored with inspiration, and to know the unknowable. In short, kundalini allows you to be *you*—and encourages others to be themselves.

Shall we see why the ancients taught about this power since time began? Why teachers, gurus, and saints across time and around the world have utilized it? Why even science is now validating its existence? Then let's open the door and step across the threshold. Let's embrace this divine energy and enjoy a truly divine life.

Brilliance in Your Body

What is this masterful, brilliant energy called kundalini?

In Sanskrit, *kundalini* means "life energy." Known as the serpent energy in Hinduism, the first culture known to have labeled this mysterious force, kundalini is the natural divine energy inside of you. *Your kundalini is the life force of your body that, when fully activated, leads to living as an enlightened sage.*

Etymologically, the word *kundalini* can be broken into the following Sanskrit roots, each of which sheds more light on what exactly this divine energy really is:

kundalin = coiled, spiraled (from the word *kundalam*, which means "ring" or "coil")

kun = earth

di = can mean "little pot of earth" or "a single cell"

and its alternative root:

da = to give or "the bestower"

lini = perpetual consciousness expressing in alpha and omega, or beginning and end

The sum total of these phrases adds richness to our understanding of kundalini. We could, based on these root words, now define kundalini as "the coiled earth energy that begins in a single cell and, when blessed by the Bestower, gifts us with consciousness."

In Sanskrit, a language in which every noun is accorded a gender, the word is feminine. This connection easily leads to the idea of kundalini as the feminine principle of creation, the life-giving properties within our physical bodies that lead to higher consciousness.[1] Our kundalini is the *yin*, or divine feminine, to our *yang*, or divine masculine. It's the receiving to the giving, the intuitive behind the logic, the contentment within the striving, and the sensual within the sexual. It's what gives us life and now sustains it, linking us with the fertile, emotional, and prosperous sources of divine energy. Kundalini compels us to feel and dance, bond and create, attract and merge. Then, when kundalini—this pulsing, creative, feminine power within each of us—joins with our male spirit quality, it sparks unity within ourselves as well as with the Divine.[2]

This feminine energy is known by many different names throughout the world, including *chi* in China and *ki* in Japan. Spiritual people might call it the "goddess within." The Christian and Jewish scriptures name it the Holy Spirit; Dr. Carl Jung calls this energy the anima. It is the source of fire in Moses' burning bush, the caduceus symbol of medicine, the life force in Buddhism, and the source of intimacy in Tantric sex. It is the serpent called Quetzalcoatl among the Mayans. In Hinduism, it is serpent power, personified as Shakti, the goddess. Most likely you have heard a few of its many other names: Al-Lat, the Great Mother, Ruah, Pachamama, Sophia, life energy, light flame, cosmic energy, divine force, spirit fire, living flame, mothering intelligence, mana, the supreme power, and Christ consciousness.

Though known by different names to different groups, kundalini is always the same force. It is the organic catalyst necessary to unify our body, mind, and soul. It is the divine light that invites poetry into our lives. It is the secret to living this human life as divine beings.

For decades, I searched to understand this power, not even knowing how to label it. In my quest, I once ended up deep inside a reservation that is home to the Bribri Indians, natives of Costa Rica. There, the local shaman worked in a shed. I had asked for a general healing but requested that he inform me about what he was doing (a friend translated for us). After following along for a while, I finally asked him the question burning on my tongue.

"What is the secret to healing?" Then I added, "I know there's a divine power, one that could change all of our lives. What is it?"

He smiled and said, "You are your own secret power. But there is an energy beyond all energies that we all share. It is here." He gestured toward my hips. "And here and here and here." He traced a finger upward from hip to heart and then to the top of my head, before finally pointing to the sky above. "All these points must come together, and then…"

"Then what?" I asked.

"Then you are One."

A light went on in my head. "Is this the same as kundalini?" I asked.

"It is," he nodded. "And it is Dios (God). And it just *is*."

Scientists might portray kundalini as electricity or as an aspect of your nervous or endocrine systems, as well as other concepts examined in chapter 5 on science and kundalini. Certain practitioners would explain it as nothing more than a means to an end, a rocket fuel to shoot the soul out of the body, while others would suggest it is best experienced through love-based sexuality, diet control, body rigors, or devoted service. Everyone seeks to enjoy its flavor, the sensual skyrocketing and spiritual bliss it brings, but when it comes down to actually defining it or explaining it…the more I've studied and researched kundalini and the more people I've interviewed about it, the more expansive and challenging its definition. I can say this, though: you have probably already felt kundalini energy for yourself.

If you have ever practiced yoga, meditated, breathed deeply to relax (or keep your temper in check), chanted or sung for spiritual reasons, used exercise to feel better, or felt a tingling when you prayed, you have experienced kundalini.

If you have participated in Pilates, tai chi, Tantric exercises, qi gong, breathwork, Zen Buddhism, mindfulness, karate or other martial arts, massage, acupuncture, or other alternative health-care practices, you have experienced the kundalini force.

If you have ever been struck with inspiration, survived a near-death experience, suffered a "dark night of the soul," been scared by a heat searing up your spine, traveled out-of-body, had a snake dream, enjoyed an ecstatic sexual exchange, or performed a super-human feat, you have experienced kundalini.

If you have experienced the pulse of a healing energy, oneness through love, or the kiss of the Infinite, or if you have been struck with a sudden surge of empathy, psychic ability, knowledge, prosperity, strength, creativity, luck, calm, wisdom, charisma, sexual charm, or consciousness, you have been blessed by kundalini.

If your spine has tingled with an electrical rush, or if the Holy Spirit, Buddha, Great Spirit, or a light from above has ignited bliss within you, you have been embraced by kundalini.

Kundalini energy is all these events and more.

The Divine Serpent Within

Worldwide, the most typical description of kundalini is as a serpent—a red, pulsing serpent of light that rises through our physical body. The first description of kundalini as such occurred in ancient Vedic and Tantric texts, which will be discussed in depth in chapter 1. In these scriptures, the oldest in the world, the serpent kundalini is considered to lie coiled and dormant at the base of our spine, in our coccyx area, until activated, or awakened. When kundalini wakes up, it primarily travels upward through our various energy bodies and channels, parts of the energetic anatomy that create and sustain our physical body. Energy is information that vibrates, and guess what the kundalini does? It shakes up the energy of our body, mind, and soul.

The kundalini first rises through energy channels along our spine. These energy channels are called the *nadis*, and as the kundalini climbs through them, it activates the seven chakras, energy centers also positioned along our spine, our center axis, and connecting our spiritual and physical selves.

Along its way upward, the kundalini must pass through three special locks, or *granthis*, as they are called in Sanskrit. The granthis are analogous to locks on a canal or riverway. Embedded in each are life lessons. (Darn those life lessons! We know all about them.) Our kundalini cannot continue upward until we unlock these granthis with the right "secret code," revealing that we have learned the lessons. These life lessons often parallel our old issues, which are held within our chakras and appear in the form of blocks. At times, the rising of our divine light can be challenging. As our chakric blocks are triggered, we must feel feelings, face beliefs, and even deal with physical problems that we've been ignoring. In this endeavor, however, kundalini is our ally. To cast a light into the darkness is to dispel the dark. How can we not come out brighter, happier, and purified?

By opening blocked nadis, owning the lessons of our granthi, and unblocking and nourishing our chakras, the kundalini activation process uncovers and heals all our hidden issues—physical, mental, emotional, spiritual, and psychological. It also opens our own intuitive gifts and encourages us to express more of who we really are in our everyday lives. So when the kundalini finally reaches the top of our spine and the top of our head, entering the topmost in-body chakra, the crown chakra, we are ready for enlightenment. Enlightenment is known as *samadhi* in Sanskrit. In the crown, or seventh, chakra, the feminine kundalini is united with her masculine equivalent, which has been dwelling in this sacred spot for our entire lives. Our full physical and spiritual selves begin to merge. In samadhi, all aspects of our true being, now fully activated by the kundalini, can achieve a state of union with the Divine and empower us to become our real selves.

In most traditions, the blended energy of the masculine and feminine, our united physical and divine selves, now shifts down to reside in the sixth chakra, also known as the third eye. We now see reality through eyes of light, and through practice actions, we transform reality into light. We have now become a participant in a divine marriage, the merging of not only our feminine and masculine selves but also our physical and spiritual essence. How could we not want to search for this same connectivity outside of ourselves?

Nearly every kundalini master offers wisdom about relationship and sexual bliss. Little wonder. The yearning we have for our selves is mirrored in the desire for another, a need to be pleased but, even more importantly, to please. Throughout this book, we will address this draw to sexual and sensual unity and various ways to embrace it.

Kundalini on the rise can produce physical effects such as heat, cold, tingling, chills, or even gentle waves of sensation. It can also trigger all sorts of nonphysical reactions, including spiritual bliss, altruistic tendencies, a desire to change one's life, or unexpected abilities or behaviors, from singing to psychic talents. Kundalini can also mirror symptoms traditionally associated with psychological or physical problems. When our reactions to a kundalini rising become too stressful, uncomfortable, or even painful, we must then reach out for help and slow down or temper our kundalini-rising process. Chapter 3 describes the various symptoms or effects of rising kundalini and offers suggestions for how to work (or cope) with them.

Kundalini may activate naturally or spontaneously, catching us unaware. We might cultivate a kundalini awakening with deliberate practice, using Eastern or even Western techniques, guiding it upward a step at a time. We might participate in ceremony, receiving the gift of this divine light through transmission from a guru. It might burst upward, only to fall down again, leaving us breathless, or reach the summit and then sit at the plateau, taking a long vacation break. We might spend the entirety of our lives watching our wristwatch, awaiting the show of the kundalini, or we might be born with a partial or full access to this feminine power. Not everyone experiences a kundalini rising—or needs to. Some individuals are already the sages they are meant to be. For some, a kundalini awakening would deter rather than add to their lives. Chapters 4, 6, and 7 explore some means of gently awakening kundalini and preparing ourselves for its rise, if it's meant to be, so you can cultivate your "garden" for this divine snake in the simplest and most joyful ways possible.

But know this: you can't do kundalini wrong. The Divine has a way of knowing what we need and offering it to us.

What Kundalini Can Do for You

As mysterious, magical, physical, sacred, enlightening, and informative as kundalini might be, it exists for a single reason: to be used. It exists to be used in everyday life for health, for relationship, and for work. It's a divine light here to shine on who you are and in all that you do. In that it unifies all aspects of you, it links you with life everywhere. You could say that to participate in kundalini is to sip from the communion cup of the Divine.

Ever since whispering a wishy-washy yes to the kundalini's first hospitable call to me, I have watched this energy change my life. I once focused my own kundalini power to write a five-hundred-page book in three months. I've employed it to chase off an attacker, and I still utilize it daily to keep up (almost) with two sons, five animals, and a house that doesn't clean itself. As an energy healer and intuitive consultant, I've watched, awestruck, as the kundalini taps into the promise latent within my clients. I was overjoyed to watch a man who had been slowly dying of diabetes become healed almost overnight, and another client, unemployed for six months, become a recipient of a healthy income source.

The most profound rewards of kundalini activation include:

- A dynamic desire to improve one's health
- The embrace of sexual energy and its sacred power
- The cultivation of self-control
- The transformation of temptations into joyous actions
- The healing of old issues
- An invitation to integrity
- A summons to spiritual purpose
- Dazzling confidence
- Heightened awareness and love of bodily needs, from relational to sexual to dietary
- Bolstered psychic gifts
- Unity with the Divine

Yet I know that because of the kundalini, we are able to do so much more. This is the power that Jesus used to raise the dead, divide a few fish and loaves into servings for hundreds, and calm a raging storm. This is the energy that gurus use to heal the sick, lower their body temperatures, and pull coins out of the air. This is the force that Australian aboriginals summon to instantly repair broken bones or track a path across the windswept desert.

Amazingly, this is an energy that we all have. Ancient knowledge lingers in the blood of each of us, as does the wisdom that knows how to embrace and respond to this native force. You've only to understand the kundalini to beckon it through the doorway between heaven and earth, and you've only to beckon it to reap rewards from it.

The goal of this book is to bring you that needed understanding. It provides stepping stones linking the classical or traditional teachings of kundalini with the needs of now, and it also reveals ways to assuage the challenges of its intense magic. And it shows you ways to benefit from your own kundalini transformation. My sources include not only the most ancient of texts and well-known of kundalini masters and contemporary scientific sources but also my own and my clients' life experiences. And if I could be so bold, I would like to think that, at times, I'm being instructed from the kundalini itself, for as physical and concrete an energy as kundalini is, it is also an aspect of the living flame we call the Divine.

This divine light pulses within us all, speaking to and through us, igniting a torch through the darkest of times, serving up joy and love in the most touching of moments. As the kundalini lights your way, know that it will share even more freely with you, being the source of inspiration that makes a difference between a "regular" life and a divine one.

Awakening
✳
in the Light

part 1

Uncoiling the Light:
The First Teachers,
The First Teachings

On the way to God the difficulties
Feel like being ground by a millstone,
Like night coming at noon, like
Lightning through the clouds
But don't worry!
What must come, comes
Face everything with love
As your mind dissolves in God

—Mystical song from Kashmirian Tantrism

All great knowledge began with great teachers. What makes a true teacher a speaker of truth is his or her closeness to the Divine. Around the world, we cherish the wisdom imparted from on high: the insights that decrease suffering, shower us with love, and reveal a path to the heavenly.

Our current reflections about kundalini, the divine life energy, originated in the same way as has every powerful philosophy. They were initiated by the celestial, passed to teachers worthy of the name, and inscribed by followers longing to live in truth. While the concepts of kundalini can be found in cultures around the world and across time, the most noteworthy information is recorded in Hindu scripture.

To understand kundalini and its effect in your life is to comprehend its first teachers and their most important points. It's to visit the holy space in which the word was first conceived and its most important scribes were born, and to follow the thread of time forward to today, covering specific teachings and ideas related to the rising of this serpent force. While the most vital descriptions are couched in ancient words, we will update their definitions so you can become better acquainted with the meaning of these terms and why the related concepts are important in your everyday life. You don't need to get lost in the language of yesterday, for truth is eternal—as are you, the conveyor of the divine light of kundalini. You've merely to tap into their meaning to find yourself nourished by the wellspring of life.

A Story from On High

The story of kundalini starts on a mountain. Attach your wings of light and fly upward with me, back through the mists of time, to seek the earliest of truths. It's okay to be excited as we land above the Indus Valley in an area now known as East India, where the Hindu version of kundalini, the bestowal of the divine light customized for the physical body, is about to unfold.

This is the summit upon which the Divine manifested in four ages of humankind, decreeing wisdom needed for all. The people of the first age, or Golden Age, delightedly and quickly inserted this knowledge into their lives. They understood the joy of living as divine beings in human form. There was no illness, trauma, or suffering, no guilt about sex in relationship, life's pleasure, and heartwarming love. Life was good, and kundalini, the energy of divine light, cleanly pulsed through each and every person, linking them with his or her divine self as well as the greater Divine.

Then trouble struck, and humans forgot their innate goodness. The Silver Age was ushered in. People still embraced the truth of being divine, but their comprehension was a little tarnished. The Divine simply smiled, as might a parent of an errant child, and took a new form. Shimmering on the sacred mount, the Divine bestowed the secret teaching yet again. The people who embraced this knowing of the Divine lived solid lives. Unfortunately, not everyone followed the precepts of divinity, and soon nearly everyone rejected the kundalini wisdom—the truth of human divinity. Once again, darkness fell, and so began the Bronze Age.

Sighing, the Divine again shared the sacred teachings, the truth of the body as a holy temple for light. But things went even worse than before; what had been dark was now black, and love became lost in the nightmares. Saddened, the Divine watched the curtain fall and awaited the opportunity to initiate the teaching once again, this time in the beginning of the fourth age, called the Iron or Kali Age, the one that we now dwell within. (This name is not to be confused with the prehistoric Iron Age referenced by historians; rather, it is a 432,000-year time period for spiritual development.) This knowledge was received by wise men called the *rishis*, as well as women with shamanic skills.

The divine insight needed for today—for our crowded, hectic, disconnected lives—was recorded in three main philosophies: the Vedas, Tantra, and the Vedanta. It is these three bodies of knowledge that those who yearn for love and hope turn to, even now. Within these three tracts, we explore for truth—the truth called kundalini.

The Kundalini Cradle: The Vedas,
Tantra, and the Vedanta

Most of us know our birth date. If our mother was a little unclear from all the stress, the moment of our entry is recorded on our birth certificate. Ancient knowledge of kundalini was certainly born a long, long time ago, but the exact time—and kundalini's human parentage—is a bit cloudy.

We do know that the roots of this knowledge are grounded in the area now known as India and are networked among several traditions. Some experts track the idea of kundalini back to the Upanishads, or "secret teachings," of the East Indian Hindu religious texts, which are dated at approximately 400 BC. These scriptures are usually called the Vedic, a term also associated with the people of that region. Other clues lead to earlier Buddhist teachings or even yogic practices from the Pakistan of 3300 BC. In the Indus Valley, archeologists have discovered a prehistoric image of a figure performing yoga; this carving has been claimed by both Tantric and Vedic traditions, seen by most to be the main pillars of kundalini teachings.

You may not have heard of the Veda people or the Vedic scripture, but the word *Tantra* is fairly well known. Most often, it is linked with sex, and "Tantric sex" outlines formulas for reaching the highest peak of the orgasmic. Can you guess the name of the energy fueling this intense sensual pleasure? That's right. It's kundalini.

While kundalini is certainly a divinely inspired source of physical pleasure, Tantra aims at much more than achieving the sexual high. As we'll explore, most contemporary Tantric sects minimize the importance of the orgasmic, emphasizing personal growth instead. Long ago, Tantra was really a shamanic tradition, a melding of various Asian beliefs and practices, with some Buddhist influences. In general, it is characterized by an acceptance of both body and spirit and the goodness of each. Many experts consider the Tantrists to be the first acknowledgers of kundalini. Close to nature and the natural processes of the physical body, Tantrists were in the position to notice and revere a body-based energy such as kundalini.

Other historians ascribe the inception of kundalini knowledge to the Vedas, the ancient Indian scriptures that were the first to codify yoga and knowledge of kundalini into writing in about 2000 BC. According to legend, these scriptures, the oldest on earth, were unveiled by the Divine to several holy men, or rishis. As you might have inferred from the story of the ages at the beginning of this chapter, these teachings are communiqués from an earlier epoch, and they reveal the best ways to achieve communal peace, personal enlightenment, and good health. Typically, kundalini practices stemming from the Vedic tradition emphasize the release of the soul from the body. Because all yoga practices, no matter what they are named, grow out of the Vedas, they all are rooted in the concept of kundalini.

Tantric and Vedic practices are intertwined yet distinctly separate approaches to kundalini energy and its regimens. Time has interconnected these two traditions, and although they were both born before the written word, there is no way to know which was the earlier practice. Between the two, there are many points of conflict and agreement. Some Tantrists reject Vedic tenets; others simply think Vedic tenets are too complex for today's culture. Some who follow the Vedic tradition refuse the authority of the Tantric system. In his review of Tantric literature, historian Maurice Winternitz points out that while the Indian Tantric texts are not completely hostile toward the Vedic tradition, they offer a more approachable doctrine.[3] As far as I'm concerned, the major differences between the two are:

- The Vedic path seeks to liberate the soul from the body and to train the mind.

- The Tantric traditions embrace the body and encourage connectivity with all.

The Vedic and Tantric traditions are like fraternal twins, sometimes raised together, sometimes separated for long amounts of time. Actually, the Tantric tradition is parallel to the Vedic system. It is impossible to examine the one without reviewing the other. Both systems embrace kundalini energy as one of the keys to reaching the practitioner's aspirations.

And some experts believe there is a third kundalini philosophy, the Vedanta philosophy. Those that follow Vedanta teachings hold somewhat unique ideas about the divine light of kundalini.

No matter which path you find yourself traveling or exploring, kundalini is always the sacred feminine, and her ultimate goal is always the same: the dissolving of self into the oneness of all.

The Vedas

As noted earlier, yoga originated with the Vedic sacred scriptures, the oldest religious texts of Hinduism, around 2000 BC. In its earliest forms, yoga was a philosophy characterized by rituals aimed at overcoming the limitations of the mind and ego and connecting with the Divine through prayer, ritual, and song. As it developed, meditation and guidelines for living, including how to treat others and ourselves, became parts of yoga. Physical postures and exercises—the main focus of most of today's yoga classes—were originally designed to prepare the body for meditation, and these have become a component of almost all modern versions of yoga.

Then, beginning around 800 BC, during a time known as the pre-classical yoga period, yogis (yoga masters) began to probe the hidden powers in the body, and many yogis mention kundalini energy in their writings. The main teachings were recorded in the Upanishads, which means "sacred revelations." Several types of yoga can be traced to this time period, including bhakti yoga, emphasizing loving devotion; karma yoga, reflecting selfless action; and jnana yoga, concentrating on loving contemplation. Each of these yogas incorporated kundalini as a way to achieve a higher end: lifting the human condition to a state of divinity.

Starting in the second century AD, yet another era, called the classical yoga period, ushered in newer understandings of kundalini. At this time, the yoga master Patanjali composed the Yoga Sutras, a benchmark text for achieving enlightenment. His work features the important Eightfold Path of Yoga, reflecting eight steps to enlightenment. Thus was birthed hatha yoga, which employed—and still teaches—these eight steps as ways to encourage the kundalini upward so we can attain spiritual bliss, or samadhi, and longevity. These steps include various *asanas*, or postures; *pranayama*, or breathing techniques; relaxation; and cleansing.

The last major developmental stage for yoga is called the postclassical period, which basically started after the introduction of meditation by Patanjali. The Eightfold Path of Yoga jumpstarted an intense interest in using yoga to prolong life and rejuvenate the body.

Another important type of yoga, still practiced today, was started by Yogi Bhajan. Called kundalini yoga, it is a systematic practice for cleansing the body in order to raise the kundalini. It incorporates many of the eight steps, including postures, breathing, and meditation, as well as visualization and affirmations. Tantra yoga also became popular, adding rituals and mantras, with an ever-greater emphasis on kundalini practices.

Ancient Veda ideals still dazzle us, even in modern yoga study— or for those of us at home exercising in front of the television. Because of our ancient teachers, we now embrace many health-conscious and personal growth–oriented practices, all of which employ kundalini as the life force that energizes the body, mind, and soul. These practices emphasize relaxation, exercise, breathing, diet, positive thinking, and meditation. What started atop a mountain is still very alive today here on earth.

In general, the Vedic path explains kundalini as a feminine, divine energy that, when merged with the masculine spiritual energy, "shoots us to the sky," lifting our soul out of the body and claiming it for the heavens. According to Vedic philosophy, any technique that directed the mind toward God was considered yoga, not only the types of meditations or exercises performed in yoga studios today. As long as the technique bestows the experience of divine consciousness, it is yoga.[4]

Tantra

As mentioned, there is a version of Tantra that coaxes the kundalini up the spine so that we can reach the heights of sexual pleasure. (We'll share a few of this version's secrets later in the book.) Even these techniques, however, are more than just titillating advice in women's magazines or the stuff boys giggle over before their mothers catch them. Tantric sex, when employed, is not only a way to reach the stars or prolong orgasms, but it is also a way to create intimacy and raise the kundalini for spiritual reasons. While the body loves to feel kundalini through sexual ecstasy, and sensual enjoyment encourages its climb, Tantra is actually a religious philosophy. Some Tantrists don't even engage in the recreation of sex at all.

Tantra has two formal paths: celibate Tantric traditions are known as the right-hand path, and the sexual tradition, the left-hand path. Even that compartmentalizing is a bit misleading, as Tantric practices have developed across Asia and emerged as divergent and multifaceted streams of thoughts and practices around the world, including Tibetan Buddhist Tantra and a classical Hindu Tantra.[5]

In all its variations, Tantra presents a divine performance and invites us to participate. The two main characters are as fascinating as any Shakespearean partners. The primary female lead is the goddess Shakti, the feminine power, or kundalini. Her male equivalent—for all great dramas are love stories—is Shiva, the male god. Shakti's ascent through the body is the maiden's pilgrimage to her holy grail and consort. In turn, Shiva's awaiting for his love is the basis of legends.

Tantra is also the name of the Tantric scriptures that explain the worship of Shakti and relay the spiritual practices and rituals aimed at achieving rebirth and liberation from ignorance.[6] All Tantra involves the activation of kundalini energy as a way to unify the female Shakti with the male Shiva. Considered separate and distinct, these two gods are nonetheless interconnected. Just as the Divine is never truly separate from us, although we might perceive it so, Shakti is never truly separate from Shiva. To help us recognize this truth—to clear our inner eye so that we can view the real nature of the universe—a pantheon of other goddesses and gods are used to assist in the recognition of our true qualities and the unconditional grace that streams everywhere in and around us.

Most Tantric practitioners employ several practices aimed at connecting with the Divine and empowering themselves magically. Participants often undergo a lengthy training process to better summon and master the kundalini, the creative force that culminates in almost miraculous abilities. Processes include asanas, or postures; *mudras*, or hand gestures; visualization; breathing; meditation; the use of mantras, or tones and repetitive words; the engineering of *yantras* and *mandalas*, or powerful symbols; and conscientious monitoring of the diet and other physical needs. Practices can also include the controlled manipulation of sexual energy, whether within oneself or in the context of a relationship. Very few Tantric practices involve undisciplined sex. Chapter 11 explores most of these Tantric practices in more detail as means of cultivating kundalini awakenings and working with rising kundalini.

What do all of these processes have in common? Tantrists believe that managing the body and natural forces invites union with the cosmos and the Divine. Consequently, many of these methods involve invoking a deity whom the practitioner seeks to emulate. Ultimately, every Tantric method seeks to merge Shakti and Shiva, for the Divine is both feminine and masculine, although in this world, we too often separate them. To leave one out is to forget a part of ourselves. It's also to pretend that we don't know what we really know inside. We already understand what the Divine taught—and is still teaching—on the mountain. We came from the Divine, and therefore we *are* divine. Is the highest goal of life not, then, to embrace our kundalini, our divine light, and live the divine life? Shine a light on a Tantrist, the fraternal twin to the Vedic, and this is the motive beneath.

The Vedanta

Some believe that there are actually three paths to kundalini and the ultimate goal of yogic practices, which is unity with the Divine. To the Vedic and Tantra traditions, they add the Vedanta.

Vedanta is a Hindu name for part of the Vedic texts known as the Upanishads. The term *Vedanta* literally means "the appendix to the Vedas." The philosophy was not crystallized until around 200 BC. By the eighth century AD, the use of this appendix had transformed into a movement of its own, one supporting personal inquiry and self-realization. There are many spinoff groups, but primary to each is the belief in Brahman, or the supreme spirit, and the desire for oneness with this creator. The two main tenets of Vedanta are that (1) human nature is divine, and (2) the aim of life is to realize this fact.

Perhaps the most well-known adherent of the Vedanta approach is Swami Vivekananda of the Ramakrishna Order. Vivekananda's precepts influenced a number of famous people of the twentieth century, including Mahatma Gandhi, Jawaharlal Nehru, Subhas Chandra Bose, and Martin Luther King Jr. His appeal could be summarized in his logic:

- God is absolute, but the world is relative. We must, therefore, pay attention to the world.

- We must remove poverty so people can turn their minds toward God.
- All religions are striving toward the ultimate truth. We should, therefore, support religious tolerance between and inside all faiths.[7]

Vivekananda's views on religious tolerance are visionary, making the Vedanta approach a truly ecumenical one. He considered women to be the equal of men, saying, "There is no chance for the welfare of the world unless the condition of women is improved… The principal reason why your race has so much degenerated is that you have no respect for these living images of Shakti."[8]

Regarding the internal Shakti, the kundalini, Vivekananda did not reject it, but neither did he consider kundalini an end unto itself. He believed that you had to first search for God and then for the "occult powers," one of which is kundalini. In other words, kundalini is supposed to be used to support one's path, not be the point of it.[9] Like the Vedic and Tantric approaches, the Vedanta explores the use of kundalini energy, but unlike them, it does so secondarily.

The most popular Vedanta yoga practice today is called Advaita Vedanta. It is a path of self-realization, inviting the initiate to move ever inward. Other types of Vedanta yoga are included within the Tantric tradition; these are Vedanta versions of bhakti, raja, jnana, kundalini, and karma yoga.

The Junction of the Three Paths

In my own view, we can put the three yoga paths together to form a complete one. By incorporating the most powerful processes of each path, we take the best of each and not only encourage the rise of the kundalini and its ultimate union in divinity, but also discourage the most irritating side effects of the awakening process, namely the stirring of "the issues," blocks caused by others' energy or by our own inner wounds.

Each of the three main avenues of the traditional kundalini paths invites the kundalini to operate in a different way.

We can turn to the Vedas to learn how to clear our mind, develop self-control, and free ourselves from energies that harm us. The more self-managed we are, the better we are able to separate our own issues from issues that aren't ours, own our mistakes, and be who we really are. Our self-esteem increases as we sort through the issues and invite the beauty of kundalini to show us how truly amazing, brilliant, and powerful we really are. Here, kundalini teaches us that we don't have to take on darkness to perceive—or help others see—the light.

We can turn to the Tantric to enhance our greater self. The Tantric stream of knowledge creates unity. Through Tantra, we explore our own inner feminine and masculine. We then embrace both, becoming more than we've ever been. The resulting bliss is one we can share with others, bringing joy into the world. Through Tantra, the kundalini shines light on our true self and prompts us toward our spiritual mission.

We can turn to the Vedanta path to explore every pocket of our being and awaken our unique attributes. That issue we've been overlooking? That emotion we've avoided? That talent we've forgotten to express? We can't merge with another until we've accepted all that we are. Through the Vedantic beliefs, we tap open and nourish each aspect of our individuality, the special learning and abilities that are ours to offer the world. Through this pathway, the kundalini nurtures every single part of us, wounded or not, and helps us heed their various messages. We become one with the circle of life.

We could say that taking a unified approach to kundalini unblocks and harmonizes us at every level. It throws open the gateway to the original heavens, the loving place from which we all come, and unbolts the locks to our desired future. We can now sing our song in concert with others so as to join the chorus of the Divine. Our lives are now bedazzled.

Sanskrit: The Chorus of Kundalini

In order to sing our unique song, we must not only understand our own internal language but also learn how to communicate with the people around us, as well as with spiritual guidance. Little wonder our primary knowledge of kundalini was first recorded in Sanskrit, the most complete and arguably most sacred language of all time.

Sanskrit is the world's oldest-known systematic language and the tongue of ancient Hinduism. References to the Sanskrit language date back to the eighth century BC, well before it was used to write the Vedic, Tantric, and Vedanta texts—the first writings that mention kundalini—and other classical literature of the Indian subcontinent.[10] The richness of the Sanskrit language has never been matched. NASA has recognized it as the only "unambiguous language" in the world, meaning that every sound, nuance, or tone has meaning, leaving one able to describe the slightest of details.[11]

The Australian website *Transpersonal: A Plain Man's Transpersonal Psychology*, written and published by Christopher Wynter and Fiona Tulk, offers the following breakdown of the Sanskrit word *kundalini*:

Kh = a dot (black stone); hollow, aperture (sometimes symbolized by the open vagina), the cup; the yoni as the feminine symbolized

U = the moon calling to the sun

N = wave (as of the ocean), ebb and flow of consciousness

Dh = virtue, merit…

A = the concept of going inward, within, or in; the feminine of the first sound (*sruti*, hidden), from which all words are formed and from which all life emanates as a bidirectional action

Li = to adhere and to hold; to rock, pulse, sway, tremble, vibrate

N = the lotus plant, the pearl, the primal mother, seed, naked

i = to pervade as perception or consciousness, to go beyond, to grow, to evolve[12]

When I found this list of syllabic meanings, I was astounded at how the meanings of each letter or sound of the Sanskrit word captured just about every aspect of kundalini I'd learned and experienced over years of working with this vital energy. I believe that kundalini's essential attributes are conveyed in these Sanskrit syllables. *Kh*, *a*, and *n* are direct references to the feminine. The letters *u* and *n* are metaphorical references to feminine energy; the moon is a common feminine symbol because women's menstrual cycles, like the full cycle of the moon from full to new, last thirty days, and the sea and its tides are directly influenced by the moon. *Dh* encapsulates the inner spiritual work prompted by a kundalini awakening. The syllable *li* seems to capture the feeling of kundalini's movement; people who have experienced kundalini risings often describe feeling inner physical sensations such as trembling or vibrating (see chapter 3). Finally, *i* refers to the expansion of consciousness that comes from kundalini's rising. Who knew that so many meanings and truths could be hidden within—and then uncovered from—a single word?

Closer to the Source: The Magic of the Divine

In paring down the term *kundalini*, we find a world of meanings, jigsaw puzzle pieces that form a sparkling image—one that is more like a colorful work of art or stained glass icon than a simple cardboard picture. To truly understand the divine power of kundalini, it's helpful to break down its energy in a similar fashion. To do that, let's explore the concept of *prana*, or life force.

A kundalini awakening and rising occurs via relationships between our feminine serpent power and our prana. Prana is considered a universal energy that animates all physical matter, including our body. Hindu, Tibetan, and Tantric yogis have directed this energy for good health and creative service, but they have also used it to perform supernatural acts such as lowering their body temperatures, performing healing, and materializing objects. (See chapter 5 for more of the miracles of prana.)

As a concept, prana is not limited to the Indus Valley in prehistoric India. China has several words for it, including *li*. Chinese legend says that long ago, li was used to power technology that could fly and enable supernatural healing. Today, we are more acquainted with the Chinese term *chi*, which exists as supernatural, mental, and physical energies within our bodies. The Japanese use an equivalent term, *ki*, which is credited with the supernatural feats of the ninja and ronin warriors. Ki also flows through all our bodies to enable health, balance, and higher consciousness.

This energetic force is known by other names in various localities, such as *kachina* in Hopi, *wakan* in Lakota, and *orenda* in Iroquois. Egyptian lore tells of a time when individuals could move great blocks of stone with rods empowered by this energy, and Canadian First Nations tell of a secret society that built great big cities and flying machines powered by this energy. Serge Kahili King, a Hawaiian *kahuna*, or medicine man, tells us that the Polynesian word for this energy is *mana*. King also employs the term *vril* to explain this energy. Scientific evidence shows that this vril has been used throughout the Polynesian culture for healing, levitation, telekinesis, fire walking, and shape changing.[13]

Prana is present everywhere in the cosmos, as well as everywhere in our bodies. In the body, it takes five basic forms, called *vayus*, which move in five different directions or serve five different functions:

1. **Prana** is chiefly located between the navel and the heart. Some texts link it mainly with inhalation; others with both inhalation and exhalation. This energy travels upward.

2. **Apana** is the descending vital energy associated with the lower half of the body (below the navel) and with exhalation.

3. **Vyana** (meaning "through-breath") is the vital energy that circulates through the limbs.

4. **Udana** (meaning "up-breath") enables our physiological functions and our ascent into higher states of consciousness.

5. **Samana** (meaning "mid-breath") is localized in the abdominal region and connected with the digestive process.

From a yoga perspective, the most important vayus for kundalini processes are prana and apana. Underlying breathing, they influence kundalini's vertical movements. Kundalini awakens when these two vayus mix and unite, creating enough pressure to force the kundalini to rise. The unification of these two vayus usually occurs through a combination of pranayama (yogic breathwork) and the use of bhandas, kriyas, asanas, mudras, and mantras—all of which we'll discuss in chapter 6 as methods for cultivating a kundalini awakening and working with rising kundalini. Some people actually force a kundalini rising by using a technique that reverses the upward flow of the prana and the downward flow of the apana.[14]

One of the great debates in the spiritual movement is figuring out the exact relationship between kundalini and prana; in fact, the words are sometimes used so interchangeably, it's hard to discern whether kundalini and prana are the same or different forces. The answer is going to be yes, no, and both.

Some experts believe that prana is an energy within kundalini—that kundalini, as a divine light, contains the prana, although the prana within it percolates, supports, and boosts the kundalini flow. Others insist that kundalini is a type of prana—that prana is an overarching energy similar to li, chi, ki, and the like, containing the feminine force of kundalini. Perhaps both concepts are true.

We might consider that, when inactive—like when it is dreaming at the base of the spine—our kundalini is smaller than or incorporated within our life force. After all, if we depended on the full flow of kundalini to be alive, many of us would be dead or sleeping all the time. Obviously, some sort of vital life force is keeping us kicking, and that would be prana, which draws on the whispering support from the sleeping kundalini. Once the kundalini begins its ascent through the body, it picks up speed. Prana, along with other energies, now nourishes the kundalini. As our kundalini's "dimmer switch" is turned up, the kundalini becomes more conscious, and so do we. When kundalini merges fully with the sacred masculine, we become our own life force; we become life.

As confusing as some of these concepts can be, they are nonetheless real. They describe the "real reality," the spiritual world that lies under and weaves throughout this physical one. Of course, the chair you sit on is "real." If not, you'd be on the floor right now. What holds your chair together? For that matter, what creative forces manifest your thoughts, tickle your feelings, and fill your soul with the gems of truth? Plain and simple, the answer is energy, or information that vibrates. It's the subtle or quick energy that composes kundalini and the various energy apparatus used by your kundalini in its upward climb and stretch to the stars. You can only fully express yourself once your energy centers and channels are bedazzled with kundalini.

What are these energy centers and channels? What do they have to do with the kundalini ascension and the unfoldment of your soul? Let's fly a little farther, this time to the stars, and see.

chapter two

From Stardust to Stars:
Does Anyone Have a Ladder?

*Like fish, reptiles, birds, and certain hardworking,
short-lived insects such as bees and dragonflies,
but unlike most other mammals, human beings
see in color.*

—Manlio Brusatin, *A History of Colors*

There's a song that coaxes children (and some weary adults) out of bed in the morning. The main phrase is something like this: *It's time to bend and stretch and reach for the stars.*

With kundalini, we can reach the stars without playing make-believe. Since time began, poets, diviners, and lovers have known that we are made of stardust, and so do modern physicists. This stardust glitters inside and around us, sometimes disguised as musty thoughts, confusion, and negativity, but just as likely appearing as dreams, desires, and love. To transform the dull or broken parts of our life, we must resculpt and reshape the stuff of dust until finally, we emerge as the brilliant star that we are—and not just a monochromatic or monotone star. We are each

33

a star of multiple colors and songs. It's not enough to only ponder the stars, however—not if you want to actually become one. We have to get in there and "get real."

There are four basic stages involved in this artful process, and I'll introduce these later in this chapter, continuing on with a true exploration in our next few chapters. As you'll discover, these steps form a rather crooked and circuitous trail to enlightenment. They twist and bend not because they are convoluted, but because the path to divinity doesn't often progress in linear or even circular fashion. In fact, the ladder to enlightenment might have been constructed by a child—and a rather happy-go-lucky, meandering one at that. The good news is that if it is approached with humor and maybe a manual like this one, the process can be fun.

Easing through the kundalini transformation—which includes dealing with our old issues, updating our current life, and living in spiritual truth—is easier if we understand that enlightenment is all about energy, which composes both the star and the dust, or the magic and the work. In turn, this celestial energy is formed into centers, channels, and even fields that coax the kundalini upward and are themselves altered through the enlightenment process. The point of this chapter is to explain these stellar energy forms inside (and outside) and shine a light on how they interact with our kundalini. I think you will discover that we actually have—and are—everything we need to reach for the stars…and actually transform into one.

The Stars in Our Paint Box

We reach the stars through four main steps, which, as related to kundalini, can be labeled *purification, awakening, rising,* and *integration.* Starting at the end of this chapter, we will devote considerable press time to these vital steps, which are packaged with a warning label: they aren't sequential. We might jump to one and then slip back to another. We might forget one altogether and have to make up for it on the next round. We might find ourselves undertaking all four steps at once and becoming quite exhausted for the trying. Some only need to conduct one or two steps, as more isn't required to lead a fulfilling life. But no matter what we're doing, we will eventually paint a new reality, one that combines the colors of the sky and earth with the gifts of our soul. Every single step (and the spaces in between) occurs through and is inspired by the energy system in and around us.

There are several terms known to the kundalini expert, and each term describes some part of this energetic process. The most well-known phrase is probably this: *kundalini awakening*.

You might not have been asked yet if you have "had a kundalini awakening," but if you hang around enough massage therapists, yoga participants, enlightened spirits, and metaphysical travelers, you probably will be. The term *kundalini awakening* denotes the activation of the kundalini and its advancement from the base of the spine upward. It sums up the complete metamorphosis of your body, mind, and soul in the shift from "normal" to "enlightened." To be normal isn't bad or wrong; it simply means that you haven't yet fully embraced the fact that you are a divine being living in a human experience. To understand how to live as light in a shadowy world is equivalent to being joyful no matter what is happening, to see and encourage the Divine in self and others, and to create more love on this planet.

The word *awakening* is really a misnomer. How many times do you actually spring out of bed, ready to rise and shine? I don't know about you, but a goodly (or godly) amount of caffeine is necessary to put so much as a smile on my face, and even then, I'm not moving much the first hour or so. Awakening our kundalini is similar to getting up slowly and carefully in the morning. After creaking to our feet, we might sit around for a while before we're really ready to rock and roll. Even then, we're not consistently going to skip through the day. Dorothy on the yellow brick road we are not.

No matter how fast, slow, joyful, or cranky our kundalini progress, it all happens within the roadways and gas stations in our energetic anatomy, the systems that convert our subtle, or fast-moving, energy into slow-moving, or sensory, energy, and vice versa. The main energy structures are called the chakras, nadis, and granthis. The auric fields, which surround the body, are another component of the human energy system. As you learn more about these various energy systems, know that you are essentially learning more about yourself, for everything is made of energy—even you.

Chakras: Wheels That Turn

The word *chakra* means "wheel of light" in Sanskrit, and that is exactly what a chakra is: an energetic wheel of light that helps steer us through life.

Even though you didn't study chakras in high-school anatomy class, these energy organs are as important to your well-being and health as your physical organs are. The main difference is that your biological organs are situated completely in your physical body. Your energy organs, including the chakras, linger in between "here" and "there," or concrete reality and spiritual reality. As the kundalini passes through your chakras on its way to the top of your head, it ignites each one. This triggers long-held issues and deeply hidden problems, but it also clarifies and clears negative energy so your inner light can sparkle for the entire world to see.

We could really say that chakras are energy converters. Located in the spine and associated with a particular endocrine gland, each chakra is able to transform fast-moving energy to slow-moving energy, and back again. Fast-moving energy could be called psychic, subtle, or spiritual, and slow-moving energy could be labeled sensory or physical. Chakras are important, because they provide a communication between these two parts of our nature, the spiritual and the physical. Each chakra manages not only the physical systems located near it, but also a set of emotional, mental, and spiritual concerns. For instance, the first chakra runs our adrenals, coccyx area, rectum, and genitalia, and it also serves our primal needs. If our first chakra is healthy and balanced, we will feel safe and secure. If it's out of kilter, we might experience anything from lack of money to an abusive sexual relationship.

The seven in-body chakras emanate from the spine, starting with the coccygeal, or tailbone, area. This is the home of the kundalini, the place it lies dormant until its time to awaken. Slip upward, and there's yet another chakra in the abdomen and subsequent chakras in the solar plexus, heart, throat, forehead, and, finally, the top of the head. This top chakra is called the crown; reaching this chakra is the goal of the rising kundalini energy.

How is a chakra able to function this way? While pictured as a wheel of light, a chakra is really more like a band of energy that vibrates from the inside of the body to the outside of the body. It attracts, interprets, and disseminates energy that correlates to its particular vibration, or set of frequencies. The red band of energy, or first chakra, communicates only with "red" energy. The second chakra? It's orange and communicates with "orange" energy. If you were to look at your chakras through energy eyeglasses, you would *ooh* and *ah* with delight. Each chakra would look like a swirl of iridescent energy, a pot of paint within a larger palette. You'd feel compelled to dabble and speckle the world with every color. That's really the job of the kundalini: to help you spread your light—and all the hues of it—through purposeful living.

There are dozens of energy and chakra systems, many professing various numbers of chakras. Some refer to a certain chakra as pink instead of blue or purple instead of white. Each system portrays chakric functions a little differently and attributes different gifts to the same energy center. Because much of what we know about kundalini comes from the Hindu Vedas, or scriptures, I'll describe the seven basic in-body chakras as seen in the Hindu system. I personally incorporate the Hindu system into a more extended twelve-chakra system, but my understandings of these seven basic

Chakra	First	Second	Third	Fourth	Fifth	Sixth	Seventh
Color	Red	Orange	Yellow	Green	Blue	Purple	White
Sanskrit Name	Muladhara	Svadhisthana	Manipura	Anahata	Vishuddha	Ajna	Sahasrara
Location	Hips	Abdomen	Solar Plexus	Heart	Throat	Brow	Crown
In-Body Connection (Gland)	Adrenals	Ovaries or testes	Pancreas	Heart	Thyroid	Pituitary	Pineal
Attribute (Spiritual Gift)	Patience	Purity	Radiance	Contentment	Unity	Command	Consciousness
Theme (Life Issue)	Physicality	Emotions	Mentality	Relationship	Communication	Vision	Spirituality

chakras are identical to that of the Hindu. The "extra five" chakras included in my own teachings are described later in this chapter, as I believe that their energies complement and expand the traditional kundalini effects.

The facing chart outlines basic points about each of the seven main Hindu chakras, including its Western name, color, Sanskrit name, and location or connection point to the body (an endocrine gland). Also listed are each chakra's main attribute, which signifies the spiritual gift inherent in each chakra, and theme, or life issue, regulated by each chakra.

Around Us All, the Auric Layers

Have you ever seen pictures of saints with lights around their body or images of angels with coronas and halos around their heads? Every time I teach a class, at least one of my students describes the colors seen around my body or the bodies of fellow students. Some individuals are gifted at seeing this bodily light, and it's this ability that prompted painters, artists, and illustrators throughout history to show the rest of us what we are really made of. We're not all angels and saints—at least not yet—but we are all shimmering beings of light.

One of the many structures of light we're composed of, the one that surrounds each of us, is called the aura. The aura is a blend of different bands of light that encompass every living being, even plants and animals. Searching the Internet, you can easily find photos of the auric fields around flowers, dogs, and, yes, human beings, proving that the artists and spiritualists of yore really were right: we are made of energy on the inside as well as the outside. When seen as a whole, the aura appears like a rainbow. Each layer is really its own field, which is the reason the aura is also called the auric field.

As an energy field, the aura performs several important tasks: filtering, separating, and protecting. Each of our chakras corresponds to one of the auric layers, which means that our chakras and auric fields work together. While your chakras run the inside of you, the auric field regulates the outside of you. Basically, the aura shares information from your body and chakras with the world, which then attracts the energies most suitable for you.

If a chakra has a block, so will its corresponding auric field. If you hold the belief that you deserve to be treated badly, the associated auric layer will allow bad energies into your body. As you clear your chakras through the kundalini process, you also clarify and heal your auric field. Without even thinking about it, you begin to screen out negative situations, people, and events, and attract positive ones to you.

As the kundalini rises, it stimulates each chakra, one at a time, along with the related auric field. This stimulation prompts the cleansing of the chakra and its companion field. As each becomes clearer, our inner self begins to glimmer and shine through our aura. The world responds to us accordingly, delivering our needs to our doorstep and attracting opportunities for growth and love. Kundalini is, therefore, an inside *and* an outside "job."

Nadis: The Paths Through the Chakras

As it rises through the body and chakras, the kundalini flows through a series of energy channels called the nadis. The word comes from the Sanskrit root *nad*, which means "movement," while the term *nadi* means "stream." Now you have a fitting picture for the nadis: streams of energy that wind through the body, carrying subtle energy to and from the chakras. As the kundalini winds upward, it carries prana, or life force, with it, energizing both the body and the chakras.

Nadis are comparable to the traditional Chinese meridian system, and many practitioners believe that they are one and the same. The not-so-subtle differences in the systems include the number of channels in each. There are twelve major meridians in traditional Chinese medicine, although there are many secondary ones. Depending on which text you refer to, there are anywhere between 1,000 and 3,500 nadis—so many that to try and visualize these energy channels would be to see the body as a design of intermingled long spaghetti noodles. Tibetan and Ayurvedic traditions, the latter an East Indian modality, agree on 72,000.[15] Another suggested difference is that meridians interact with the duct system, and the nadis with the physical nervous system.[16] Whether or not the meridians and nadis are identical pathways, both deliver subtle energy and assist with the productivity of the physical body.

The central nadi, the *sushumna*, passes through the spinal column, serving as the main highway for the rising of the kundalini. As the kundalini leaves its home base, the chakra at the base of the spine, it travels through this central channel but also diverts through two other nadi streams, the *ida* and the *pingala*. The ida, actually starting below the first chakra and ending in the left nostril, is considered a feminine channel. It is thought to assist us with conserving energy, increasing serenity, resting the mind, and boosting our psyche. The pingala is masculine in nature. Also initiating below the first chakra, it conveys prana and our kundalini all the way to the right nostril. It is associated with power, vitality, quickness, and constructive actions. (Some schools of thought reverse the flow of the ida and pingala, especially during the early stages of a kundalini awakening.[17])

The chakras are nourished by the kundalini as it stimulates the ida and pingala, but there's also another outcome. Kundalini stirs our spiritual gifts, the divine attributes that lift us to the stars but still secure our feet firmly on the earth, the place we are called to serve. Ultimately, kundalini illuminates our divine being. Better able to see ourselves, we can also better see others and their true divinity. In short, kundalini awakens the gifts of each chakra and promotes better health, both physically and spiritually.

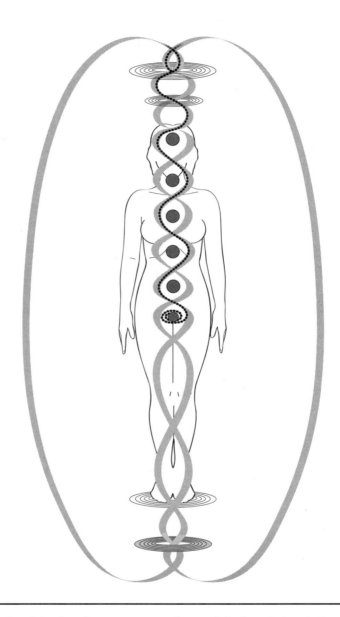

The kundalini lies dormant, wrapped around the first chakra, before awakening. It then climbs up the three main nadi: the ida, or feminine, on the left; the pingala, or masculine, on the right; and the sushumna, or central, spine, before merging with her masculine and spiritual counterpart in the seventh chakra.

This caduceus, or symbol for modern medicine, first appeared as the staff of Tehuty, the legendary high priest in Egypt, who brought "divine knowledge" of sacred healing. It was also claimed as a sign of the Greek healer Asklepios, who healed through the subtle currents of the body as well as by encouraging the "spiral windings of the soul's evolutionary path." Here is pictured the kundalini; the ida, pingala, and sushumna; and the joining of the feminine with the masculine. In cultures across time, healing requires the awakening of the physical energy of kundalini and its marriage with the spiritual energy inborn to us all.

Of Locks and Blocks

As I hinted, kundalini doesn't always flow easily or consistently. The actual process reminds me of the time I visited Panama and observed the Panama Canal, the only land-based conduit between the Atlantic and Pacific Oceans. If you can't go through the canal, your ship has to struggle through 8,000 additional nautical miles around the tip of South America, a trip that will incur you more expense and danger.

To take advantage of the canal, ships must await the filling and release of three locks, which must operate like clockwork. Having slipped through one lock, a ship is positioned for another, and the next, and then onward until its time to traverse the open sea. But beware! Slipping through the locks is not always that easy. There are storms, trials, and tribulations on either side of the canal. Other potentially challenging factors include the seaworthiness of the vessel, the fortitude of the captain, the attitude of the sailors, and even the quality of the ship's food. All in all, there is a series of locks, or blocks, that must be overcome or cleared to ensure a safe voyage through the Panama Canal.

The kundalini passageway is similar. To pass from our "normal" to "enlightened" state, our kundalini must navigate three energetic locks and deal with a lifetime of concerns. The locks are called *granthis*. Placed near three different chakras, each granthi is encoded with a certain lesson that must be learned, or we'll be deadlocked. As well, our chakras hold energy blocks, representations of the physical, emotional, mental, and spiritual issues that disguise our true nature. They do so because they store everything we've ever been through, as well as our own editorial comments, or negative beliefs, that we create in reaction to life's ups and downs.

How does kundalini trigger the locks and the blocks? Kundalini is a master at discerning truth from falseness. A divine energy, kundalini wants a tidy ship and is willing to push until each and every obstacle is out of the way. This is why so many people groan at the thought of a kundalini awakening, and why so many gurus suggest a preparation period to the rising stage. A ship can travel to, through, and from a canal easier if there aren't any logs in the way. But life isn't always evenhanded. While kundalini discharges our blocks, sometimes the opposite occurs. Life events can also activate our blocks and, in turn, stimulate a kundalini awakening.

Does this mean we should stay safe in the harbor and avoid life's potential dilemmas? We'd certainly have fewer issues to deal with, now, wouldn't we ... or would we? The divine life is fulfilled by human experience. We are enriched by every aspect of life, from the good to the bad, the hard to the easy. In fact, it's not our life events that create our problems; it's the conclusions we draw from these events. Trauma, including abuse, accidents, or loss, is horrifying and creates upheaval at every level. Life dramas affect everything about us. When we're able to deal with tragedy as it occurs, we eventually adapt to resulting changes and continue with our lives. We might never be the same, but we transform and grow in a new way. Sometimes, however, we form conclusions that impede our forward progress. For instance, if we are raped by an African American man, we might deduce that all "black men" are bad. We won't take a job where African Americans work or live on the same street as "someone like that." We've formulated a belief that hurts not only us, but also others.

Our personal philosophies, as well as taught beliefs and modeled behaviors, are stored in our chakras. As the kundalini rises, it triggers everything—and I mean *everything*—that doesn't correlate with our true self. This includes physical illness, dysfunctional beliefs, stored emotions, and spiritual misperceptions. If we are willing to face our issues and work through them, we invite freedom from the related oppression and eventually uncover our true self.

One client I helped in this way came to see me because she was losing a lawsuit against a drunk driver. He refused to admit his guilt. For her part, she was making excuses for his insincerity, refusing to testify directly against him. Her own insincerity was literally hitting her in the heart—she had developed an intense pain in the thoracic area, a section of the spine in back of the heart. Why wasn't she stepping forward and sharing her truth? She didn't want to insult the drunk driver. "I don't want to hurt his feelings," she said.

I sensed that there was a little more to her story, and so I asked her to reflect backward to a time in childhood when she'd been told not to tell her truth. My client's spine immediately went into a full spasm, a searing pain emanating from her coccyx to her injured vertebrae. Wondering if we were dealing with a kundalini rising, I asked her to stay with the pain for a minute or two and to share whatever memory came up.

My client told me that at age five, she was forced to read a Christian tract about how to manage anger. Why? Her mother used to beat her on the back with a spoon whenever my client—a little girl—would say something that the mother didn't like. The mother became most vehement if my client would confront her about a lack of integrity. (And my client was the one with the anger management problem?) While sharing this story, a red line of energy visibly emerged on my client's back, from her coccyx to the thoracic. When assured that she did, in fact, deserve to be angry with her mother and, in this instance, at the drunk driver, my client began to cry. The red line disappeared, as did every stitch of back pain, which was replaced by what my client described as feeling like a "golden line of light" that rose from her coccyx but now went straight up her spine to tingle at the top of her head.

My client was exhibiting a kundalini block, a heart-based resistance to recognizing her own goodness. As every chakra manages its own set of concerns, each also stores specific types of blocks.

The first chakra typically reflects misperceptions and fears about our safety and security, which often manifest as serious life issues, addictions, job confusion, financial lack, and terminal or chronic health problems. When the kundalini comes calling, the second chakra reveals emotional and creativity challenges, while the third chakra shares issues regarding self-esteem, personal power, and work success. Kundalini climbs to the fourth, or heart, chakra and triggers love and relationship topics. In the fifth chakra, it stirs up questions about communication and our ability to say what we really think or need. Up it rises into the sixth chakra, where concerns about self-image and the future loom, and finally, in the seventh chakra, we find issues about spirituality and our life mission.

When rousing these chakras, troubles and blocks related to the physical glands and organs in the related area might also manifest, though, as suggested, a life event can trigger the inherent issue, calling the kundalini to the scene. Once there, the kundalini inflames the stuck problem—not to create harm, but to help us clear the blockade once and for all.

In classic kundalini teachings from Hinduism, three of the chakras' energetic blocks are identified as especially important: those of the first, fourth, and sixth chakras. We deal with not only the chakric blocks but also the special challenges of the granthi, or energetic locks, located in or near these chakras. Just as the locks on a canal must be opened to allow ships to pass, these energy locks must be opened so the kundalini can continue its winding path upward to the seventh chakra. Each lock has its own set of symbols and invites its own particular set of teachings, which are the secret codes that must be figured out in order for the kundalini to move forward through the lock. Learn the lesson, and onward you go.

These three locks and their lessons are:

Lock/Granthi	Chakra	Typical Chakra Blocks	Lesson
Brahma	First	Childhood abuse issues; financial challenges; addictions; repressed sexuality and identity confusion; questions about primary partner, lifestyle, and career; potentially fatal illnesses; greed, envy, and materialism	Release ourselves from the trappings of material world and establish the self in totality
Vishnu	Fourth	Questions about lovability, deservedness, relationship needs, codependency, separateness from Divine; heart, lung, and breast conditions	Perceive the existence of universal life principle
Rudra	Sixth	Issues with appearance, self-worth, and body image; questions about future, goals, and dreams; challenges with vision, perception, learning, and hormones	Release duality and realize oneness with joy

What happens when the kundalini is unable to pass through either a granthi or chakra block? We experience reactions, from physical maladies to emotional outbursts. The knot of the granthi must be completely unwoven for the kundalini to continue on. (Perhaps it's a good thing that there are only three such locks.)

Regarding chakras, the good news is that only part of a chakra is actually affected by—or infected with—a block. There are two rings composing every chakra. These look like the rings of Saturn. The outer ring of energy is programmed with our soul issues, life concerns, and maladaptive responses to life, but the inner ring is programmed by our spirit and contains all the codes we need to lead a good and healthy life. If we can access the spiritual energy from the inner chakra circle, we invite divine healing, perspective, and change. Because each granthi is located near a chakra, we can tap open the light in the inner wheel of the associated chakra and receive divine inspiration for healing the misperceptions in that granthi, as well as the chakra.

The Benefits of Unblocked Chakras

As the previous section tells us, each chakra contains more than just blocks and bad memories; each is also laden with gifts, bright and shiny. As the kundalini passes through each of the chakras, it might trigger our issues, but as those issues clear, we experience incredible gains as well. The equivalent is this: turn on a light in the dark, and you can not only see what needs to leave, but also what can be received. When kundalini runs into our chakra blocks and energizes our healing process, it opens space for us to receive the benefits and gifts inherent in each chakra.

Now we're having real fun. Sort of like responding to our holiday shopping list, the kundalini is able to attract what we really desire in our life. Through the first chakra, located in the hips, you can gain more money and financial prosperity, a greater sense of your own identity, and healing in your physical body. These things come to you not only because the kundalini invites the release of security blocks and fears, which stand in the way of our primal needs, but also because it magnetizes the related auric field to draw what we desire to us. As our deeper self-worthiness issues clear, we experience more vim and vigor, closer personal relationships, and a more fulfilling and intimate sexual life. We also face—and can heal—adrenal stress, rectal and other excretory disorders, and life-threatening addictions. Passing through this chakra and corresponding lock signifies that we've fully owned our right to exist, the love of our body and the physical world, and, ironically, the priority of people over material objects.

Through the second chakra, grounded in the abdomen, kundalini triggers a release of pent-up emotions, both yours and others', and a resulting boost in creativity and innovation. As others' feelings clear, we experience more clarity about our own needs and, ironically, greater compassion and care for others. Codependent urges are confronted and overcome, expanding an appreciation of our five senses and our body. Problems with eating disorders, premenstrual syndrome (PMS), and intestinal issues can now be dealt with and healed.

The third chakra, located in the solar plexus, encourages us toward success and acceptance of our personal power. The kundalini strikes by first stirring up our fears, negative beliefs, and self-esteem issues. Just wait—you'll survive. As we face our judgmentalism, we embrace greater work success, an increased ability to establish and maintain a serviceable life structure, and the healing of digestive issues, nervousness, and memory problems.

The fourth chakra is based in the heart, the center of love and healing. The kundalini, upon reaching the heart, now triggers the corresponding granthi and our own relationship issues. Can we open to unconditional love? Learn how to give it? Passing these "tests" allows us to believe that we deserve love, to the point of being able to care for others and ourselves. Healing might now occur for conditions related to the heart, lungs, breasts, shoulders, arms, and chest.

The fifth chakra, located in the throat, governs our communication skills. The kundalini loves to activate the negative or self-destructive "old tapes" that enter through the backside of this chakra. Upon responding, we're able to transform destructive beliefs from Mom, Dad, and society so we can hear ourselves, express our needs, and listen to others with love. Kundalini awareness promotes the healing of throat, neck, jaw, and teeth problems.

The sixth chakra, situated in the brow, is the center of vision. As the kundalini works, we are asked to peer in the mirror and see ourselves clearly. This examination usually ushers forward parts of us with a low self-image, those imaginings preventing us from perceiving our true beauty and worthiness. Upon perceiving our true selves, we begin to transform into the self we really are, healing inner and outer vision issues, learning disabilities, coordination problems, and pituitary and hormone imbalances.

The seventh chakra, based in the top of the head, serves higher consciousness. The seat of our spirit and the entry point of the

Divine into our bodies, this center enables spiritual insight. As the kundalini merges with this spirit center, we experience oneness with the Divine and an awareness of our soul aspirations. Potentially, we receive healing for headaches, mental illness, insomnia, neurotransmitter disorders, and general confusion.

The Gifts That Reach the Stars

For a moment, let's return to the sacred mountain, the residence of the Almighty. Is the Divine female or male? A god or a goddess? You can't figure it out, because as soon as you scrutinize, God plays the Cheshire Cat and all you see is a smile hovering in the air, then a great big eye winking at you. Now you hear a laugh, and a coin flashes out of nowhere to land at your feet. (Hmm, is it possible to get maybe a bag of these golden doubloons?) You reach for the coin, but the Divine is on to new tricks. A searing beam of light strikes you in the chest, and you are immediately transformed into light. Your concerns drop away before you transform back again into a person. That same intense light now pours from your hands, and you know that you can heal others. In fact, you can do almost anything: make a coin appear, see beyond the horizon, maybe even shape the horizon into a picture postcard. What's happening?

You are experiencing the gifts of the spirit, the Divine made manifest through the human self. You are practicing a few of the gifts that might arise through a completed kundalini transformation.

Divine energy operates at a different level than physical energy does. It's quicker than regular light. It doesn't have to obey all the traffic cops of the universe, those that insist you dig a trench before you leap into joy or work a job before making money. As the chakras, in particular, clarify and transform, something magical begins to happen. The gifts inherent in each chakra, those that support your specific and special spiritual mission, start to activate.

Every culture professes a certain set of miraculous gifts. In the Christian community, they are the fruits of the spirit; in aboriginal cultures, they are often called medicinal or shamanic abilities. In the metaphysical world, they are considered psychic phenomena. In Hinduism, they are termed the *siddhi* and defined as godlike capabilities that turn on through the kundalini enlightenment process. If or when they do show up, these gifts don't appear out of nowhere. They are seeded within the chakras, from conception onward.

Energetically, each chakra houses a certain set of these gifts, many of which lie dormant until kundalini awakens them. Through the kundalini process, we are freed from earthly constraints, fears, and shackles and shouldn't be surprised to find ourselves more intuitive, experiencing different ways of knowing, understanding, sensing, and being. As the kundalini clears away debris, our innate gifts are able to shine. Always there, they now come into our conscious awareness. We are now able to fully use them for good, to meet the higher purpose we are on this planet to achieve. If, at times, your kundalini process gets you down, remember it's only doing so in order to lift you up. There's always a higher plan, even if we can't see it in the moment.

What might these gifts look like? Following are descriptions of what the siddhi might look like in our "normal" existence:

> First-chakra abilities concentrate on physical empathy, the ability to sense others' physical conditions in your own body. As the kundalini rises, this sensitivity transforms into the ability to manifest material needs for ourselves and others. For instance, we might feel compelled to start a new company or to make or manage money in a different way.

> Second-chakra gifts center on feelings and the ability to sympathize or empathize with others' emotions and emotional needs. As the kundalini clears out this chakra,

we become free from the codependent tendencies to take on others' feelings and ready to develop our creative, compassionate potential. Most people apply these gifts in one of two ways: by serving in a therapeutic role for others or by exploding forth as a creative genius.

Third-chakra capabilities include mental quickness and clairsentience, the ability to sense information from and about others and the world at large. As the kundalini hones our skills, we are better able to serve in administrative and organizational capacities, applying our intelligence and intuitive knowledge to support a higher mission.

Fourth-chakra capacities are heart centered, which is another way to say they are relationship based. A wide-open heart is able to give and receive healing for self and others.

Fifth-chakra gifts are communication oriented. On the psychic level, they include the ability to receive spiritual guidance, channel, perform automatic and guided writing, and the like. The kundalini upgrades these gifts so we can access higher spiritual principles and divine knowledge, and then share these with others through verbalization, writing, and music.

Sixth-chakra gift attributes are visual, summarized in the term *clairvoyance*, which means "clear seeing." A higher-functioning sixth chakra allows us to accurately perceive the past (as in, looking through God's eyes), choices embedded in current reality, and fixed or potential futures. By visualizing a preferred future, we can set about manifesting it.

Seventh-chakra talents are spiritual in nature. Before a kundalini awakening, they enable spiritual knowing, or the sensing of the Divine's presence and heart, as well as the ability to sense others' current levels of consciousness and integrity. Through the unification of the feminine kundalini and the masculine spirit in this chakra, these gifts explode in brilliance. They could be summarized as prophetic: the ability to animate the Divine's mission on earth.

These siddhi, or talents, aren't limited to the descriptions listed here. There are as many gifts as there are people on this planet. Part of the fun in opening to your kundalini is discovering exactly how gifted you are.

Flying Farther: Beyond the Seven In-Body Chakras

Have you ever thought you had just a few of something, only to discover you actually had more? This concept isn't enjoyable if the objects in question are dust bunnies or bills, but what about realizing that you had more money than you thought—or more chakras than you might think?

The seven-chakra system is the one most taught in the Western world. This makes sense, as we are a body-based people and are seldom trained to sense or see beyond the physical. For decades, however, I've worked with a twelve-chakra system, following in the footsteps of Eastern, South American, and even African traditions that add anywhere from one to nine chakras to the in-body seven.

The following "extra" five chakras are located just outside of the body, even though each is physically linked to the body. I have found that employing these chakras for kundalini clearing and yogic practices can greatly aid the purification and healing processes involved in a kundalini awakening. It also affords the activation of several additional spiritual gifts, which means that we're suddenly able to fly higher and more frequently in our life pursuits.

On page 56 are brief descriptions of these additional chakras and a few notes about how activating their gifts can benefit us.

These higher, out-of-body chakras allow us to access energies not normally available when pulling kundalini only through the body. One of the energies available through the expanded chakra pantheon is a masculine counterpart to the feminine kundalini. This "masculine kundalini" is similar to that discussed in the Vedic, Tantric, and even Buddhist systems. These three systems say the masculine divine is housed in the seventh chakra, but I establish its haven in the ninth chakra, a gold energy center way above our head—and nearer to the heavens than our brain is. Understanding the feminine kundalini necessitates comprehension of its masculine counterpart.

Let's Get Together: DFE (Divine Feminine Energy) Seeks DME (Divine Male Energy) for Love and Enlightenment

This is the day and age of the personal ad, the searching for intimacy and a life partner through the Internet. How might the feminine kundalini compose such an advertisement?

Divine light of God, very feminine, loves red—red clothes, shoes, and accessories. Enjoys great food, a good time, striving for higher service. Once roused from slumber, ready to go. Looking for equally vibrant guy who loves honest conversation, dancing in the light. Must be seeking perfect union.

Living the divine life requires the merging of both sides of the Divine—namely, the female and the male. The kundalini rises to seek her consort, her mate, her lover. Our kundalini transformation isn't complete until this happens. Exactly how this happens—or which lovers play what part—depends on who is telling the story.

In the Vedic tradition, the goal of kundalini is to rise to the seventh chakra, where, through the clearing of seventh-chakra issues and the activation of that chakra's gifts, we are able to achieve union with the Divine. The emphasized outcome is a somewhat asexual intercourse between self and the Divine; the chakra itself is thought of as nonsexual, although three faces of the male divinity

Chakra	Eighth	Ninth	Tenth	Eleventh	Twelfth
Color	Black, power for movement, force behind change	Gold, harmonizes and draws God power to a situation	Brown, practicality and grounding	Rose, shifts supernatural and natural forces	Clear
Location	Above the head	An arm's length above the head	One and one-half feet under ground	Around body, hands, and feet	Around entire auric field
In-Body Connection	Thymus gland	Diaphragm	Bones	Connective tissue	32 in-body connection points
Attribute (Spiritual Gift)	Shamanic capabilities, including abilities to soul travel to other planes, dimensions, and aspects of time	Harmonizing, the ability to sense the needs of the world and summon the divine powers needed to create peace on earth; can also "read" the genes of our own and others' souls, those symbols that make each person unique, and current life purpose	Naturalism, the ability to perceive the needs of the natural kingdom, perform nature-based healing, and communicate with beings in the natural world	Can summon and direct natural and supernatural forces, from the wind to powers from other planets	Unique to each person
Theme (Life Issues)	Karma, release of the past, opening to imaginative possibilities, visiting other planes and dimensions, connection to the deceased or people who might be in your future	Harmony, opening soul powers and gifts, can access the siddhi that match soul purpose, enables service to the world	Grounding, ancestry, and the earth	Leadership through interconnectivity	This chakra represents your personal path and individual spiritual gifts, those that lead to fulfillment of your higher spiritual mission

dwell within it. These three forms of God are Shiva, the god of destruction; Brahma, the god of creation; and Vishnu, the god of maintenance; all of which unite, once the kundalini integrates, in the form of Lord Dattatreya. These individual figures represent the three fundamental powers of the masculine, existing perpetually.

Although Shiva's realm is usually associated with violence and pain, Hinduism says that Shiva invites us to pay attention to what has enduring, rather than transient, value. Brahma suggests that subtle energies are more powerful than physical ones. No one can control the universe, but by seeking truth, we can shape the universe inside and outside of ourselves. Vishnu lights the pathway to truth. His love is especially important in our times of crisis and darkness. Ultimately, Vishnu's teaching is that we each carry a light, a torch that can illuminate the way for others and ourselves. Combined, these three divine forms merge with the feminine kundalini to marry us with the Divine.

In the Tantric tradition, however, there is usually only one strong masculine figure: Shiva. Upon arising, the feminine kundalini, Shakti, unites with her masculine counterpart. There are a few more fireworks and flares in this version of the kundalini story, and followers are encouraged to embrace the divine feminine and masculine inside of themselves—in some traditions, through intimate relationship.

There is yet another adaptation to the love story between Shakti and Shiva, and it is my own, which is based on years of cross-cultural research, spiritual study, and client observation. In contrast and as a complement to the red serpent kundalini, which is feminine, I perceive a male kundalini. I call it golden kundalini and consider it comparable to the Shiva energy of Tantric practices.

Both feminine red kundalini and masculine golden kundalini are based in the energetic body. While the feminine kundalini lies in the first chakra (and is why this kundalini is seen as red), the masculine kundalini enters the body through the ninth chakra, which hovers an arm's length above the head and connects to the body via the diaphragm. Gold is the color associated with the ninth chakra, which means that the masculine kundalini is also golden in color.

The best way to understand the golden kundalini is in contrast to its feminine partner. The feminine, red kundalini, as known to most traditionalists, clears and empowers your chakras, as well as your physical and emotional energy. The masculine, golden kundalini represents your soul energy, as well as higher spiritual and mental forces. The red kundalini rises or climbs up; the golden winds down. They eventually meet, blending the highest of celestial truths with the most organic of earth energies.

The red kundalini, the red serpent, which rises from below, is hot, sometimes searing. It livens you physically, emotionally, and mentally, sometimes setting off issues you would really rather not acknowledge, but must. The golden kundalini, which falls from above, contains no hint of danger. Flowing along a river of pure divine light, the golden kundalini is personalized energy that initiates your soul in body, accentuating your life purpose and spiritual gifts and opening you to divine blessings. Bringing these two kundalinis together is another gift of a kundalini awakening. Together, these two kundalinis merge not only feminine and masculine, but also earth and heaven, physical and spiritual, soul and body.

What compels the golden kundalini to descend from on high? It often lingers in its heavenly haunt until its feminine lover arises to the seventh chakra, at which time, upon spying its matching partner, it hurries to the meeting ground of the seventh chakra. This is the most typical way golden kundalini descends. Sometimes a spiritual experience persuades the golden kundalini to drop into the body whether or not the red kundalini has started its upward climb. If the golden kundalini, without its complement, completes its own cycling through and around the body, it continues to revolve until its feminine lover is ready to mate. In this case, your life will be overly spiritual and lack practical grounding.

Sometimes the two kundalinis initiate their journeys at the same time. This sudden influx of two kundalini powers can be jarring, especially if it occurs instantaneously or too quickly. I believe the most life-enhancing kundalini process involves the gradual introduction of both the red and the golden kundalinis at the same time, usually leading with the golden.

Even more effective is to introduce what I see as a third type of kundalini. Called the radiant kundalini, it is, in some ways, even more brilliant than the other two. Chapter 7 explores radiant kundalini in more detail, and I'll give you my own personally designed method of using it to cultivate a safe awakening of your divine feminine.

Stages of the Kundalini Coming to Life

As stated in the beginning of the chapter, there are four basic stages of a kundalini transformation. These are:

1. Purification, the preparation of the body for kundalini's glide upward;
2. Activation, or the actual kundalini arousal;
3. The rising, or the passing of the kundalini through the nadis, chakras, and granthis; and
4. Integration, living in the light.

The truth is that these four stages are anything but sequential. Many people experience a sudden rush of kundalini, sometimes out of nowhere or in reaction to a crisis or trauma. They then employ purification processes, such as diet control and breathing exercises, not to cultivate the kundalini but to survive its arrival. Others carefully groom themselves for a kundalini awakening only to realize that it has already occurred and they've actually been integrating their spiritual energy into their lives all along. Still others might not need an awakening at all, as they are already on plan with a rising.

As we proceed with the book, we'll be examining the various ways to perform all four steps according to your own particular needs. To lay the groundwork, however, I'd like to offer an excellent summary of the initial stages of kundalini from Patanjali Kundalini Yoga Care (PKYC; see kundalinicare.com), a website offering spiritual-development education based on traditional kundalini teachings from India. This thorough outline matches my own experience and can provide structure to a sometimes formless process.

No rising: The kundalini lies dormant at the root center at the base of the spine. It blocks the opening of the sushumna. This is the state in an ordinary person.

Stirring: The prana stirs, beginning to spin in the first chakra. The kundalini, though, remains in the mouth of the sushumna nadi and continues to grip the base and responds by shaking. Someone at this stage might shake, weep, dance, run, laugh, or exhibit some other sort of reaction. If the reaction is positive, the person may be motivated to repeat whatever behavior served as a catalyst.

Arousal: The kundalini uncoils and unblocks the opening to the sushumna nadi. However, the prana is usually too weak and the mind too unfocused to support a full release of the kundalini from the root chakra, so there is no rising. To change the situation, we must take on training that focuses on virtue; otherwise, the kundalini can be tempted by negativity and be pulled into the dark below the first chakra, thereby engaging in dangerous and delinquent behaviors.

Release: Uncoiling, the kundalini withdraws from the sushumna and, with enough energy and focus in the subtle system, leaves the first chakra. It can do so only if the energy system is clear and vitalized, and if there is proper mental and emotional focus. This focus is usually aroused by spiritual practices or an intense life drama. The kundalini now enters one of the available nadis and rises as far as it is capable at that time.

Once our kundalini releases or awakens, we experience any of the following types of risings:

Partial rising: Kundalini rises through the sushumna nadi and travels to the heart chakra but remains underneath the granthi. Unstable, it goes up and down between this point and the first chakra, creating fluctuations until it is ready and able to move on.

Deflected rising: The kundalini is deflected from the sushumna and takes an alternative nadi to the seventh chakra, opens the brain centers, and then falls back to the first chakra. It fails to undo the granthi in this scenario. One may experience the activation of talents and incredible spiritual experiences but frustration as well.

Intermediate rising: The kundalini rises through the sushumna nadi, passes through any blocks in the first through fourth chakras, and lands in the fifth, the throat center. It is stable and opens certain gifts, but these gifts can become overtaxed.

Full or complete rising: The kundalini elevates through the sushumna and flows upward to the seventh chakra. Various chakric spiritual gifts, or siddhi, may open. We are completely transformed by oneness. We now enter the state of integration, which lasts the rest of our lifetime. We are ready to fully integrate our experience and its gifts into our everyday life.

When the kundalini has fully risen, we have become a different person than we were before, but we also have the same life. We must now educate ourselves about the spiritual life—the one lived through everyday normality. We must learn what it is like to be both feminine and masculine at the same time, to not divorce our higher self from other aspects of our self or the world around us. We might need to recover from the rising kundalini or set new life goals.

In yoga, there are three stages of the completed kundalini awakening, sometimes called the plateau experience:

- *Shuddha beha*, purification of the physical system
- *Pranava beha*, improvement of brain function
- *Jnana beha*, refining higher intelligence

These yogic stages reflect how our brain changes once the red kundalini, or Shakti, has merged with the golden kundalini, or Shiva. Usually, we experience improved brain function and endorphin production. The symbol for the seventh chakra is a thousand-petaled lotus; each petal represents a different brain center. As these parts of our brain transform, so do we.

Most kundalini traditions hold that after the complete rising, kundalini takes up residence in the sixth chakra. From this base camp, it is able to commute elsewhere when needed, helping us release old issues and misperceptions as they arise. The kundalini is accessible throughout our energetic system and for issues and activities, small and great.

PKYC says this plateau experience, a complete kundalini rising, is the goal of all spiritual paths and can result in transformation to being a "realized sage." Once we have experienced it, we are often called to service, to help and assist others and the world.[18]

Integrating and adapting to kundalini-prompted changes is easier if we are willing to reach out for help, love, and support from others who have gone through this stage. In chapter 8, I offer my own advice for integrating risen kundalini and its changes into our lives.

What Starts a Kundalini Awakening?

A kundalini awakening can be initiated in any number of ways. Sometimes our kundalini is startled awake in a dramatic, unexpected fashion by an event, trauma, or stressful situation. Other times, it rouses slowly and gently in response to our ongoing nudges.

A traumatic event, life change, brush with death, metaphysical experience, sexual encounter, or stress or shock of some sort can trigger a spontaneous awakening, a sudden and fast uprush of kundalini. For example, I once had a spontaneous awakening following a physical attack. More and more people are surviving death experiences, which can be precursors to a kundalini awakening. In chapter 3, we'll discuss in detail the signs and symptoms of awakenings, as well as how to cope with their effects.

Kundalini awakenings can also be cultivated with years of gradual preparation. These cultivated awakenings are much more gentle and usually more comfortable than spontaneous awakenings, because when the kundalini does quicken, our preparations have helped us mature to the point of being able to handle its intensity. Cultivated awakening is the most common of kundalini-activation processes, and if you're a seeker wanting to experience the benefits of the red serpent, it is definitely the most recommended. Cultivation techniques usually concentrate on purification. Eastern practices such as yoga, tai chi, qi gong, and meditation encourage the unfolding of our kundalini. If you're involved in any of these practices, you may already be consciously or unconsciously cultivating an awakening. Chapter 6 discusses how to cultivate an awakening and offers various specific techniques from classical yoga for doing so. In chapter 7, I explain my own technique for safely opening yourself to a kundalini awakening.

Are You Crazy, or Is It Kundalini?

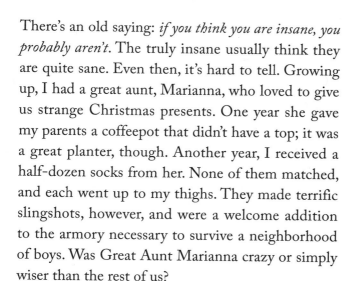

Madness need not be all breakdown.
It may also be breakthrough.

—R. D. Laing

There's an old saying: *if you think you are insane, you probably aren't.* The truly insane usually think they are quite sane. Even then, it's hard to tell. Growing up, I had a great aunt, Marianna, who loved to give us strange Christmas presents. One year she gave my parents a coffeepot that didn't have a top; it was a great planter, though. Another year, I received a half-dozen socks from her. None of them matched, and each went up to my thighs. They made terrific slingshots, however, and were a welcome addition to the armory necessary to survive a neighborhood of boys. Was Great Aunt Marianna crazy or simply wiser than the rest of us?

Having said that, sometimes kundalini can make us feel insane, which isn't a particularly comforting reaction.

chapter three

Kundalini is an energy. It is information that moves, or light that reverberates. Most people also report it as a conscious energy, and if nothing else, it does make us more conscious. Because it is a blend of matter and spirit, working within our energy system, as the collective nadis and chakras are called, it has a very energizing effect. This has earned kundalini a reputation for being a potent, strong, and sometimes overpowering ally.

Many practitioners stress that you must be ready for a kundalini awakening, or activating and working with it will endanger your health, your well-being, and sometimes your sanity. Many of these dire warnings stem from the unusual, puzzling, and sometimes dramatic reactions that can occur with an awakening, be it cultivated or spontaneous.

This chapter discusses the many and varied effects of a kundalini awakening. Because kundalini can manifest itself dozens of different ways, I've included several lists and descriptions of symptoms and signs. You'll also learn a method of distinguishing kundalini symptoms from your everyday garden-variety psychoses, as well as ways of healing and dealing with kundalini's effects.

Your Own Private Idaho: The Individual Kundalini Experience

If everyone on the planet somehow managed to live in a single geographic area—or own a piece of their own private Idaho—they would still feel like they were living in a different country. Kundalini on the rise affects different people in various ways. Yours might be activated in the middle of the night, after a healing, in a therapy session, after decades of spiritual growth, or for no apparent reason at all. The signs might be slow and gradual, almost imperceptible. Your kundalini might be alive and kicking long after you think it settled down, and you might not even know it. The combination and intensity of kundalini symptoms will be unique to you, but there are some common, classic signs.

I received a crash course in how diverse kundalini symptoms can be when, one Sunday in May, not one or three but *five* clients came to see me because they were dealing with a recent or recurring kundalini awakening.

The first gentleman was a famous musician, a singer with an incredible voice and a bevy of young, swooning female fans. He had been lying in bed a few days earlier when the lyrics for a new song sprang into his head, as if "delivered by God." Then he felt the earth shake and a voice say, "There will be more," before he realized that it was not the ground giving way, but his own body.

"For days, I've been trembling and experiencing sensations of hot and cold," he complained to me, shivering. "And all I can think of are lyrics, song after song after song." He added, "If this is a creative muse, I'd like her to go off-duty."

Another client was a mother with three children, and she had spent years being angry with her husband. Upon finding out that he had been having an affair, a "boiling energy" starting rolling up her spine, and she was now alternating between intense sexual urges and a feeling of rage.

Two of the other three clients were a bit frightened of their experiences. One man's encounter followed a long retreat in an ashram, in which he had sat in silence and devotion to the Divine. A student of yoga for years, he reported having had a series of gentle kundalini experiences long before the retreat; these experiences had included a throbbing between his spine and his crown, moments of tears and remorse, times of bliss and ecstasy, and a compelling desire to be of service. This recent experience was more intense. Bouts of white light were flashing in his head. Neurologists had ruled out a stroke or a physical cause, leaving him to wonder what the spiritual message might be.

Another individual had experienced a "bad trip" during a drug-induced state. Besides swearing off recreational drugs forever, he was willing to do anything to make good of his life, if only I could stop the guilt and moroseness that kept sweeping through his body like a "hot, searing pain." The fifth client was a young girl whose mother brought her in because, since birth, the girl would break out in a strange chanting every so often. The child's hands would then heat up, and she would pray for people. The mother had just read about kundalini and was wondering if it could be a part of what was happening.

As I worked with these individuals, I saw that kundalini and its effects were at least a part of every single experience. Because it is important to rule out other causal factors such as physical or psychological disturbances, I commonly send clients to licensed health practitioners to do just that. Because all my "mayday" clients had already done so, I was certain we were dealing with kundalini. Each person was exhibiting at least some of the classic signs of an extreme kundalini awakening:

- Tingling, itching, crawling, stinging in the body or brain, sometimes described as ants walking
- Heat or cold, pinches or burning, flushes in the skin or inside the body
- Energy running between the nadis and chakras
- Muscles twitching
- Sense of electricity charging your system; you begin to blow out lights, clocks, or electrical objects; objects knock over when you are around
- Alterations in eating or sleeping
- Times of extreme hyperactivity or fatigue
- Intensified or diminished sexual desires
- Racing heartbeat, pains in chest (you must check these out with a medical doctor)
- Numbness or pain in limbs (same as above)
- Emotional outbursts, rapid mood shifts

- Hearing inner melodies, sounds, beautiful music, or noises like ringing in ears
- Mental confusion, difficulty concentrating
- Altered states of consciousness and mystical experiences, including out-of-body projection, extrasensory perception (ESP), past-life memories, increased psychic visions, channeling, body sensitivity, a sense of altruism, healing powers, contacts with spiritual guides or ghosts
- Increased creativity; new talents or interests
- Deeper understanding of spiritual truths
- Pressure in sixth chakra; some describe this as a band, others as an internal pressure
- Seeing flashing white lights
- Sudden short-lived bursts of energy
- Spontaneous urges to perform asanas, or yoga movements
- Overwhelming feelings of love and desire for a partner (I believe the lust that some report as overtaking them, whether or not drug- or alcohol-induced, is not kundalini but rather a symptom of issues that must be worked through; see "When the Snake Is Too Sexual" later in this chapter)
- Pain in lower back or wherever kundalini feels a little stuck
- Vibration, often in the inner ears
- Spontaneous bliss and unity; awareness of the Divine
- Receiving the Holy Spirit, as Jesus's disciples did at Pentecost; as described in the Bible, receiving the Holy Spirit can result in speaking in tongues, healing abilities, experiences of the Divine, knowing of truths, revelations, visioning, speaking the "Word of God"
- Arms and legs move like a baby[19]

Since the kundalini's path takes it upward through our chakras, chakra-specific issues may also be signals that our kundalini is on the rise, as can the sudden manifestation of chakra gifts. Experiencing a sequence of issues correlating to each of the chakras in turn—first some root-chakra security issues, followed by second-chakra emotional upheavals, then third-chakra mental-clarity challenges—is a clear tip-off that your kundalini is going somewhere. Following is a list of energetic blocks within each chakra that might alert you to a kundalini transformation:

First chakra: Intense physical sensations or pain; burning in the coccyx; pain in the very low back; intense skin sensitivity or inflammations, or alternating patches of cold and hot; electrical pulses through spine or along skin; rectal, adrenal, vaginal, bladder, or similar conditions; struggle with finances, poverty mentality, or critical conditions, including alcohol or hard drugs; gambling, shopping, sexual, or other thrill-seeking addictions or compulsions; sudden craving for sexual orgasms or complete shutdown of sexual desires; intense memory recall of abuse; hyperawareness of others' physical conditions to the point of sensing or being afflicted with their illnesses or physical issues.

Second chakra: A release of long-stored feelings or a heightened awareness of current feelings; spurt of creative urges or sudden block of the same; waves of various feelings, sensations, or food cravings, especially for carbohydrates; desire to touch and be touched; oversensitivity of others' feelings to the level of feeling their feelings for them; problems with womb, testes or ovaries, hormones, or intestines.

Third chakra: Anxiety attacks; awareness of inner fears; low self-esteem or self-confidence issues; mental chatter; hyperawareness of information and data because of sensing others' inner mental life instead of one's own; problems at work or following a structure; digestive issues; caffeine, soda pop, coffee, and beer addictions.

Fourth chakra: Love and relationship issues; healing crises; challenges with heart, lungs, breasts, or shoulders; oversensitivity to others' relationship needs; codependency; nightmares or scary dreams; struggle with sugar, wine, or other sweet substances.

Fifth chakra: Communication challenges, such as difficulties with expressing the self or healing others; hyperclairaudience, such as intense channeling, transmediumship, or the hearing of spirits and voices; problems with throat, neck, jaws, ears, and teeth.

Sixth chakra: Visual issues, including hallucinations, psychic visions, spots or blurs in eyes or in the inner mind; flashes of the future for yourself or others or, conversely, difficulties planning or foreseeing the future; challenges with eyes, hormones, and balance.

Seventh chakra: A sense of the Divine or fears regarding the Divine; intense spiritual or religious experiences; desire to perform higher service; activation of miraculous abilities; intense reactions to others' lies and negativity; an overwhelming attraction to truth, integrity, and the light; unbounded optimism and cheer; sleep issues; flashes of light in the head; activation of anxiety or depression or bouts of both; awareness of spirits, good and bad.

Signs of activation of the other five chakras in my twelve-chakra system include the following:

Eighth chakra: Shamanic experiences, including out-of-body and astral projection, a sense of being in two places at once; hyperawareness of others' needs, illnesses, feelings, and thoughts; interaction with entities, spirits, and other dimensions and planes of existence; flashes into your own past lives or those of others; absorbing of others' issues and, as a result, experiencing challenges in discerning self from others; autoimmune disorders; inflammation in body; challenges with thymus or immune system; any or all addictions or addictive tendencies.

Ninth chakra: Sense of higher purpose for yourself and others; awareness of global needs or sudden draw to helping a certain group or cause; interest in or notice of numbers, symbols, or colors that provide signs or insight; issues with breathing.

Tenth chakra: A draw to nature; receiving signs and communiqués from the natural world, either in everyday life or through dreams; reactions to chemicals, inorganic substances, cosmological or geographical energies or areas, or human-made energies, such as cell phones or power lines; visitations from natural beings or deceased ancestors; problems with a house or housing; compulsion to track or understand genealogy or lineage; genetic or bone disorders.

Eleventh chakra: Interface with natural and supernatural forces or sudden jolts of the same, such as tornados or windstorms; insights into personal force or ability to command; disorders in muscles, fascia, or connective tissue.

Twelfth chakra: Highly personal, resulting in a calling to understand or fully become the true self.

Multiple Awakenings,
Multiple Effects

You might also have several kundalini awakenings, each of a different nature. This is what happened to me. My big blowout occurred in my early thirties, but subsequent smaller awakenings happened as years passed. I believe the aftershocks resulted from an incomplete initial rising, and, in fact, the granthi and chakra at my heart level had been stuck.

One of the clues to this diagnosis was that, after my first kundalini shakeup, I developed a heart arrhythmia, or aberrant heartbeat, that took years to completely dissipate. Afterward, I worked on absolutely every relationship issue ever invented by humankind, learning how to put the "kind" into the concept of being human. During many of these years, I also had white flashes in my head, and these flashes would beam all the way down to my heart. A neurologist insisted that I wasn't experiencing white flashes. I believe these flickers were helpful nudges from the masculine spiritual energy coming down from the top of my head. The heart condition and bright lights disappeared as soon as I thoroughly forgave both those who had harmed me in my life and myself, for my part in the experiences.

My own first awakening occurred right after a man tried to molest me. While I got away from the attacker, the next day, an indescribable heat began climbing up my spine. I could literally feel it hit various blockages in my body over the next couple of months. Some blocks were emotional, and I would find myself crying, once for almost seven days straight. Other blockages were physical. My neck would cramp, for instance, but it also healed almost immediately after I saw a chiropractor. Other symptoms were mind oriented. One entire evening I worried about almost everything until finally I decided that worry was a worthless endeavor. I heard a pop in my head and a voice say, "All is love."

When the most demanding kundalini symptoms died down, I was a changed person. I felt prompted to do something different with my life and also to *be* something different. I examined my diet and exercise. I looked more deeply at the romantic relationship I was in and saw how I was confining myself within it. I pursued even more travel than I had before, seeking the answers to that provocative question, "What is this all about?" And I started my business as an intuitive consultant, whereas previously I had been in marketing for a nonprofit organization.

One of my favorite subsequent awakenings occurred when I was traveling in Mexico and had the sense to stay in my room when all my friends went out. I had been feeling strange and uncomfortable all day. Finally, I lay down and began to meditate, drawing my breath up from my abdomen and practicing the nostril-breathing exercise included in chapter 6.

I heard the voice of God. He—or she—said, "It's time to choose your purpose." At the same time, I felt a "bump" behind my heart; I believe now that my kundalini had been resting there, having only partially risen before, and was now ready to proceed upward again. Without much warning, I felt rushed out of my body and found myself in a space I could only call heaven.

There, a voice spoke through an enveloping, cloudy mist. "Are you willing to heal?"

I said yes, and I was suddenly jolted back into my body.

My heart felt different, like there was more energy now moving through it. I believe that at least part of the heart-centered granthi, or lock, had now unwound. The heart chakra is about healing. As the kundalini continued to flow in and through my heart over the next year or so, I experienced an intensely increased desire to learn more about energy healing and medicine, in addition to the arrhythmic condition. I was also prompted to step up my own self-growth work, through family-systems therapy and other venues for strengthening my relationship with my inner selves, as well as with my loved ones.

Mayhem Possible:
When the Serpent Lunges

Even though we prefer to have control of when, how, and why our kundalini awakens, sometimes it just doesn't happen that way. Even the most carefully supervised cultivation process can cause kundalini hiccups in which the serpent energy rises in spurts, each bout leaving the student breathless, emotional, shaky, and feeling overextended and scared. And sometimes circumstances—or fate—intervenes, and the kundalini rises abruptly and fast, exploding us into a state of spiritual emergency.

Both the ancients and many contemporary spiritual leaders warn us that an out-of-control Shakti can leave you feeling—and being—out of control. Let's examine the potential mayhem—and magnificence—of a snake that has startled itself awake, including ways to recognize and alleviate a too-sudden, not-so-charming uncoiling of the kundalini.

Spiritual Emergency

We're all familiar with everyday emergencies: the pasta water boils over, the dog really does eat the homework. Worse are the dreaded, bigger crises—those that leave us gasping for breath: a parent goes to the emergency room; we lose our job.

Atop these is another category of emergency that's not often named: the spiritual emergency. Bottom line, it involves experiencing heightened levels of awareness or energetic trauma for which we are unprepared. We become so startled that we're unable to take care of ourselves.[20]

Discerning between a genuine kundalini emergency and other problems can be complicated. In reviewing the symptoms of a kundalini awakening, you'll see that they can be confused with other real-life issues and, in fact, are often one and the same. Just because your kundalini is causing heart palpitations doesn't mean you don't have heart palpitations. Distinguishing kundalini from organic issues can help us create the spiritual breakthrough we're looking for and deserve.

When "Too Hot" Hurts

One way to sort kundalini from other catastrophes is to categorize the kundalini signs. I know it's easier for me to create a plan if I'm a little better organized. If nothing else, by classifying symptoms, you can better approach a professional for assistance.

In her book *Energies of Transformation: A Guide to the Kundalini Process*, Bonnie Greenwell outlines seven categories of symptoms accompanying sudden kundalini activation. While some of these signs echo those listed earlier in this chapter, I think the way they are categorized here is helpful. Also, these particular symptoms relate specifically to spontaneous, or sudden, awakenings.

> Pranic movements: When the prana, or vital energy, is released suddenly, this intense energy can trigger physiological blocks. The result can be involuntary jerking movements such as spasms, contractions, and shaking. The release of these blocks can rouse previously hidden memories, emotions, traumas, and injuries.

> Yogic phenomena: Some individuals begin performing yogic postures (asanas) or hand positions (mudras) that they could not have learned in their current everyday life. They may speak Sanskrit, hear music or tones, or start chanting mantras. They may experience unusual breathing patterns or not breathe for an extended amount of time.

> Physiological symptoms: Kundalini can generate a release of bodily toxins, leading to the appearance of heart problems, head and spinal pain, gastrointestinal disturbances, and nervous-system issues. Individuals have reported sensations of burning, overwhelmed senses, hyperactivity, hypoactivity, variations in sexual desire, and even spontaneous orgasm. These indications can be erratic and may not respond to standard medical treatment.

Psychological upheaval: A spontaneous kundalini activation can challenge the ego state and the myth of our separation from the Divine. It can stimulate responses to drives and shift instincts—from ego-based consciousness to psyche-centered consciousness, for example. These changes can produce confusion, often accompanied by unexplainable emotion swings—from anxiety, guilt, and depression to compassion, joy, and love—and bouts of uncontrollable weeping.

Extrasensory perceptions: Our perception enlarges, expanding outside of our previously typical reality. The result can include visions of lights, symbols, and entities, or an awareness of past-life experiences. Auditory stimuli may include voices, music, inner sounds, or mantras. Some people experience various smells, while others lose a sense of self as a body, feel larger than the body, or travel outside of the body.

Psychic phenomena: Various psychic abilities might activate within us, including precognition, telepathy, psychokinesis, healing gifts, and the awareness of auras.

Mystical states of consciousness: We might shift into altered states of consciousness, perceiving the unity within reality. This altered state can produce experiences of peace, serenity, and wisdom. This psychological upheaval can be so great that it seems like a psychotic episode.

Hundreds of my own clients report similar and additional kundalini-related symptoms. I also have had the "pleasure" of experiencing my own kundalini awakenings—both sudden and spontaneous risings and chronically slow climbs. Based on my professional and personal knowledge, I would add the following indications of a sudden kundalini awakening to Greenwell's list:

Alteration in composition or appearance of the body: One of my clients grew two inches overnight; another person's hair color changed from brown to blonde within a month.

Loss of memories: One client lost memories of about one-third of her childhood—all the traumatic events—leaving her in a newly achieved blissful state.

Extreme changes in diet or cravings: One client shifted from an omnivorous diet to a vegan diet within a day.

Fresh sense of destiny: Several clients report being called for a unique mission and even receiving brand-new talents. One gentleman started drawing pictures of people's souls. He quit his job as an engineer to pursue this new, innovative career.

Sense of being "someone else": Several clients reported feeling that they had never been their "real selves" and were now struggling with how to assume this "true self" in their current lives.

New knowledge: I worked with a fourteen-year-old girl who got up one morning with a full knowledge of the French language. Who knows what might be awakened through the kundalini?

Gender identification issues: One client suddenly knew she was supposed to have been a man at birth and underwent a gender change, with the full support of her (now his) family of origin.

Belief that the experience will kill you: Sometimes the kundalini experiences are so strong, we think they might actually do us in. When someone calls in a panic, scared for his or her life, I first check to see if there really is a true crisis and direct the person accordingly. Often, however, the real issue is a fear of death or, conversely, a fear of life. Especially when inside or close to the first chakra, the kundalini surfaces the most primal of questions and needs, and I often encourage a direct interface between a client and the Divine to discover the meaning of life and death.

Any or all of these symptoms can be awful—and awesome. You might need trained assistance to understand if you are experiencing a clinical breakdown or a true spiritual breakthrough, as the signs can be similar. Or you might be experiencing both: kundalini can trigger a true clinical breakdown that ultimately results in a spiritual breakthrough. Consider this list, which outlines the physical or psychological disturbances often mirrored by the kundalini:

- Heart attack, stroke, or sudden onset of systems-based conditions
- Brain disorders, tumors, uremia, diabetes, infection, toxic cardiac states, hormonal challenges, and injuries
- Reaction to life changes, such as divorce or loss; midlife crisis or other transitional time periods and trauma
- Reactions to drugs, including medications or use of recreational drugs
- Psychosomatic breakdowns, including psychosis, mania, depression, schizophrenia, bipolar disorders, borderline personality disorder, paranoid states, persecutory delusions and/or hallucinations, use of mechanisms (including projection, exteriorization, and acting out) or other mental health issues[21]

So Is It Kundalini or Something Else?

How can you distinguish kundalini from "else-wise"? The key is that kundalini eventually invites the emergence of your true self, alleviating the spiritual emergency. As you emerge from the state of emergency (rather than simply living in it), you find yourself evolving, becoming more creative, peaceful, and calm. Eventually you feel drawn to concentrate on more than the crisis or uncomfortable sensations and feelings. You begin to care, not only about

Always Seek Professional Help

The onset of any intense or frightening symptoms calls for help. Just as we can't always heal or comfort ourselves, we also can't diagnose ourselves. The symptoms of kundalini awakenings can also mark true physical or mental disorders that must be treated by a qualified medical doctor. Most researchers believe that the kundalini-awakening process is not pathological but is a sign of maturation. At the same time, it is important to rule out genuine, treatable conditions and receive assistance from a trained professional.

There are a dozens of different indications of a kundalini awakening, each of which could also reference a real physical or emotional concern. Kundalini is just one potential energetic trigger of any of the symptoms described in this chapter. It's important to explore all the possibilities, including working with a qualified health-care professional, to screen out other concerns before diagnosing yourself as a kundalini initiate.

yourself, but also about others. At this point, you know that you really are here on earth at this time on purpose. You are here to serve, love, and create more love.

In other words, one of the primary ways to know if you are having a breakthrough versus a breakdown is the eventual outcome. I know that doesn't sound immediately encouraging, but think about this: no matter what you are going through or why, you can transform challenge into an opportunity.

The Kundalini Syndrome

You know what it's like. You've been looking forward to a vacation for months, and the first day has arrived. The alarm goes off at 5 AM, and you stumble out of bed, stepping on the kids' toys and injuring your foot. There go all those romantic walks on the beach. You barely make it to the airport in time before your beeper goes off. Of course, there's a work project that didn't get done—and your mother is ill, asking if you can bring her to the emergency room. Finally, just before the airplane is supposed to leave, the pilot says, "We have a malfunction. Please remain in your seat for an hour, and we'll keep you apprised of when we might be taking off."

You haven't even gotten off the ground, and "real life" has intruded.

Well, the kundalini process is the same. Even when we carefully cultivate our kundalini awakenings, we can still experience challenging effects when our kundalini begins to climb.

Years ago, noted teacher Chögyam Trungpa Rinpoche was giving a talk on spiritual development. He started by asking how many members of the group were just starting their practice. When a number raised their hands, Rinpoche said, "Fine. My suggestion is that you go back home." He explained, "It is a lot more difficult than you know when you begin. Once you start, it is very difficult to stop. So my suggestion to you is not to begin. Best not to start at all. But if you do, then it is best to finish."[22]

One of the reasons that Rinpoche was so cautious is because enlightenment transforms one's life. The process can be quite dramatic—and difficult. Awakening to our divine self via kundalini requires a bit more than showing up for yoga class, praying to God, or breathing accurately. It involves more than acting with altruism or worshiping in a sacred space. It involves feeling and healing the body, dealing with long-held issues, suffering through once-ignored emotions, examining negative beliefs, quitting addictions, eating right, and taking actions that might be new and frightening. In essence, kundalini asks us to mature on every level. For some, it calls attention to the stuck issues in remarkable and challenging ways.

A new term has arisen in response to the ever-increasing appearance of symptoms resulting from kundalini activation. This term, "kundalini syndrome," is the brainchild of theorists within humanistic and transpersonal psychology, as well as near-death studies. The symptoms calling for compassion and treatment include various physical, motor, sensory, mental, emotional, affective, and cognitive problems.

It is important to note that this syndrome is not associated with a typical kundalini rising or a single kundalini episode, such as a sudden, quick rising. Rather, this term relates to the result of prolonged and intense spiritual or contemplative practice, such as meditation or yoga, or an intense life experience, such as a trauma, a close encounter with death, or a near-death experience.

The most prominent symptom is the intense rise of energy along the spine, which usually triggers tremors, shaking, involuntary body movements, and changes in respiration. It is often accompanied by changes in body temperature, such as heat or cold; a sense of electricity in the body; headaches or pressure inside of the head; tingling; vibrations; and gastrointestinal problems. Symptoms can include psychological upheaval, severe stress, depression, a sense of nonreality, intense mood swings, altered states of consciousness, and hallucinations, but they can also include moments of peace and bliss.

The good news is that the means by which we nudged our kundalini awake—such as those described in chapter 6—often work well in helping us overcome the effects of kundalini syndrome, as do the healing methods described in the next section.

What Might Help?

What do I tell my clients who need help with their kundalini symptoms? First, I often refer them to therapists, psychiatrists, or medical doctors who understand the idea of a spiritual emergence. If the practitioner believes it would also be beneficial for the client to work with me, I draw on the following tools to provide assistance:

Regressions to remember and reframe childhood problems: Many of our issues lie in our childhood. We must rescue our "inner children" if we are to mature into the adults we deserve to be.

Regressions to past lives in order to sift through the deeper spiritual issues: I believe that past lives often establish the ground for our current life experiences. I don't encourage past-life therapy as a way of life, however. We shouldn't retrieve the past to retreat within in it, but only to look for themes to resolve the present.

Use of healing to connect with the Divine: This usually involves searching in the past for reasons clients perceive a disconnect between themselves and the Divine. Most often the issue is abandonment or guilt, the sense the Divine left you in danger or won't forgive you an error. The healing for both misperceptions is the acceptance of unconditional love and grace.

Release of energies that are not our own: I believe that up to 80 percent of our problems are caused by absorbing others' issues, including illnesses, emotions, beliefs, spiritual ideas, and even experiences. A simple way to release others' energy is to ask the Divine to take it to the rightful owner's higher self. This higher self can determine a safe or appropriate way for the energy owner (dead or alive) to work out his or her issues. It's important to then ask the Divine to fill in the remaining hole within ourselves and return us to wholeness.

Setting of energetic boundaries: Our auric field acts as an energetic boundary, determining the type of psychic data we let in, process, or disseminate. Abuse, trauma, and wounds create holes in our boundaries. After pinpointing the cause of the wounds, we must also energetically seal the energy boundaries. The Divine will do this upon request.

Elimination of energetic bindings, curses, or entity attachments: Yes, I believe in curses and all things that go bump in the middle of the night. I've seen individuals heal almost overnight upon releasing these energetic entrapments. Ask the Divine to help or seek assistance for this work.

Integration of soul fragments or aspects of the self: Trauma splinters our soul, and parts of it can lie repressed within the self, in other dimensions or planes, or even inside other people or beings. Work with a professional to help you track, heal, and place these parts of yourself back into yourself.

Activation of intuitive and spiritual gifts: We all have intuitive gifts. Each chakra carries its own gift; in fact, as explained in chapter 2, kundalini often awakens these gifts, and it's important to define and cultivate them.

Connection to spiritual guidance and protection: We all have spiritual guides. I usually help clients ask the Divine for a gatekeeper, a God-appointed guardian that shares intuitive messages and screens energetic callers.

Projection to possible future, in order to establish a new path: There are myriad potential futures. Clients love asking the Divine to show them the best possible ones so they can create a desirable life.

Making of healthy lifestyle choices: Part II of this book includes information about proper dietary, exercise, and other lifestyle changes for health and well-being. We are physical beings and deserve to take care of these beautiful bodies. Self-care alleviates many kundalini-based concerns.

Embracing of limits: We have limits. We really have to sleep, eat well, and exercise. We can't work all the time, even if we wanted to. Most kundalini-based practices help us perceive and accept the limitations that keep us healthy and whole.

While these guidelines are broad, I often find that clients must follow at least a few of them upon a kundalini awakening. For instance, I once worked with a woman whose kundalini shot open when her oldest son was killed in a car crash. Her natural devastation was compounded because she immediately began experiencing surges of heat up and down her spine. She was also plagued with daily flashbacks of a car accident she had been in as a child, and while she was sleeping, she experienced dreams in which her son appeared to her. These dreams caused her great agony, as she couldn't figure out what he was communicating.

She was already seeing a chiropractor for treatment, but I also sent her to a spiritually friendly psychiatrist to evaluate her emotional state. She found some relief in the prescription medicine, but not much. I then used regression therapy to help with the "child within" who was still cycling through the childhood car accident.

During the regression, my client remembered being hit on the head and flying to heaven, where she had wanted to stay. Apparently paradise was preferable to her family home. God had sent her back, however. She became so angry that she closed down her lower chakras, as well as her intuitive gifts. If God wouldn't bring her up, she wouldn't let him in "down here."

The loss of her son cancelled out this protective maneuver, forcing upward the life energy she'd been repressing. Her psychic gifts also activated. When she was able to calm her inner child and foster a relationship with the Divine, every symptom—all of which pointed to a kundalini experience—disappeared, save the psychic connection with her son. After I helped her accept her psychic gifts, my client was able to relate to her son, who only wanted to coax and coach her into a better life from his new home on the other side. Then one evening, he departed, telling her it was his time to dwell in heaven and her time to live on earth. She ended therapy with me, ready to rejoin humanity and live in wholeness within herself.

I have found that each kundalini client requires a different type of support, comforting, healing, and training. But I also know that every person experiencing kundalini symptoms is being assisted by the Divine. If you are experiencing a true kundalini awakening, be assured that you are already being guided and comforted. Isn't the kundalini really the Divine moving through your body? To follow the kundalini is to flow with the Divine.

When the Snake Is Too Sexual

One of the most discussed outcomes of a spontaneous kundalini awakening is increased sexuality. Unfortunately, this is the symptom that frequently gets sensationalized in the "spiritual newspapers," which often report it as compulsions, fantasies, a craving for multiple orgasms, and an unquenchable desire for sex.

I have found that any extreme kundalini symptom indicates the need to address deeper issues. In the case of overly potent sexual desires, the wounds are most likely sexual or relational in nature and often point to an abuse of power. These are usually first-chakra issues, which are often the most challenging to deal with, as they are primary and primal and beg the question of our true worth and value. Compulsive sexual behaviors might stem from sexual abuse, the misuse of sexuality, an exposure to inappropriate sex, rape, violence, or even religious judgments causing sexual repression. The drive for sex isn't usually about sex at all. It often indicates a fear of intimacy or a misapplied way to feel powerful. If you experience an overwhelming sexual desire that that interferes with your life, seek professional therapeutic help.

Be cautious about judging your sexuality, however. Some spiritual teachers or organizations teach that you can only reach enlightenment if you are celibate. While certain individuals might be called to this path, it's too extreme for most. As pointed out by Gopi Krishna, author of *Kundalini: The Evolutionary Energy in Man*, one of the first books to introduce Western readers to kundalini, there was no system of celibacy in India during the Vedic times, nor was monasticism a part of the early Christian church.

Here are a few more words of wisdom from Gopi Krishna regarding the proper use of sexual energy:

- Sex energy creates spiritual energy and can lead to more creativity.
- An excess of sexual indulgence, however, leads to lost energy and obsessiveness.
- Invite true sexual pleasure by waiting. Let the pleasure build and truly give to your beloved.
- Remember that periods of abstinence will not make you insane; sexual energy can be directed to other endeavors.
- Moderate the sexual urge; do not repress it.
- Strive for what brings true bliss—oneness with the Divine. This is the ultimate goal.[23]

Softening the Kundalini

Mantras, as we'll learn in chapter 6, are chants that soothe the soul as well as the kundalini. They can clear out the nadis and chakras and connect us with the Divine. One particular mantra, called the *Soham*, is particularly designed to clear the energy channels. Also called the *Hamsa* mantra, it asks the question, "Who am I?" The answer is *Soham*, or "I am that." Said repeatedly, the Soham mantra actually means "I am that I am, that I am, that I am." It employs two sounds:

- *Sooooo* is the sound of our natural inhalation.
- *Hummm* is the natural sound of exhalation.

It is safe to use at any time.

This is the mantra:

> *O mind, sing the sound So Ham*
> *Soham Japalehe Manawa*
> *Soham, soham, soham.*
> *I am that I am, that I am, that I am.*

You can listen to an audio version of the Soham mantra on the website Swamij.com: Traditional Yoga and Meditation of the Himalayan Masters (www.swamij.com/soham-mantra.htm).

Consciously Cultivating the Climbing Kundalini

*One is wise to cultivate the tree
that bears fruit in our soul.*

—Henry David Thoreau

Are you ready? Set? *Wait!* No matter if your kundalini hasn't fully aroused or engaged, if it's taking a nap or a vacation, or even if it's steadily plugging along, you will benefit from consciously cultivating your climbing (or still cradled) kundalini. We're talking about the first but really ongoing kundalini stage of preparation or purification.

As mentioned in chapter 2, the safest way to activate your kundalini is by engaging in practices that gently and gradually awaken it. Most kundalini-based gurus encourage students to follow a strict spiritual protocol in order to eliminate the possibility of a too-sudden kundalini awakening. Cultivating a kundalini awakening usually includes years of slow mastery of soul over mind, mind over body, and spirit over energy. This extended training period ensures

that the student has the time and space needed to locate and heal emotional blocks, deal with negative beliefs, change bad habits, and meet obligations.

As well, purification can and should be performed throughout the kundalini process, whether your kundalini has met its masculine counterpart and the marriage ceremony is already registered with the County in the Sky or you're in the middle of the motions. We are always and constantly called to care for our bodies, and yoga protocol, such as the practices described in chapters 6 and 8, is one of the best ways to do it.

One of my clients exhibited this cultivated-awakening process to perfection. A Christian, she had endured a strict family reaction to her practice of Zen meditation, working with a naturopath on her diet, seeing me for energy healing, and taking kundalini yoga classes. She also employed a mental-health therapist, if for no other reason than to cope with her family's reaction to "playing with the devil." (Ironically, yoga, meditation, and good health aren't precursors to any particular religious path. In fact, the closer we are to our true selves, the closer we are to the Divine, however we understand the Divine to be.)

One day at church, my client felt a slight stirring in her groin. She began to tremble and become hot; she wondered if she was entering early menopause. Later that day, she talked to her yoga teacher, who helped her breath her way into and through the very gentle rising of the kundalini that she was experiencing. Childhood memories accompanied the small "stops" the kundalini made along the way, and my client had an emotional but enriching day. She did not have a metaphysical experience, simply physical and emotional occurrences.

About a year later, I noticed that she began to smile more often. I asked why. She replied that gradually, her understanding of God, herself, and the world had changed. She was thinking of taking training to be a Christian yoga instructor.

Purification

Purification is a key component of a cultivated kundalini awakening. When we purify ourselves, we prepare a clear path for the kundalini, not once, but repeatedly. There are many aspects of purification and hundreds of potential ways to become clean and clear. But the most important point to understand is that purification is not about sanitizing or perfecting; it is about linking all parts of us together in love.

To purify the body is to wash, nourish, nurture, and treat it with love. To detoxify is to cleanse ourselves of pollutants because they rob us of well-being. To eat organic food is to fuel ourselves with care. To free ourselves of addictions is to say we value ourselves. To enjoy sex in order to better understand a loved one and ourselves is much different than using sex to gain a sense of self or power over another. To exercise is to worship the Divine through movement. To purify our mind is to abstain from injurious ideas and fill ourselves with supportive ones. Acknowledging that a clean mind is a happy mind means that there is certain material we cannot read, discuss, or pay attention to. These are only a few ways we may prepare for kundalini.

We are also spiritual beings, and as such we must purify our hearts and souls. We are immortal and eternal—and sometimes terribly confused. Our souls, which have existed long before entering this lifetime, carry knowledge like karma and dharma, of what we have done and what we seek to learn. (We will examine these concepts in chapter 12, as well as methods for cleansing all aspects of us in chapter 8.) Purification is both a kundalini-preparation process and an act of kindness toward ourselves.

From a yogic standpoint, purification must also include another important factor: energetic cleansing. The nadis and chakras contain everything we have ever done, said, or thought. Energy is simply information that moves. Some of the information loaded within our energy system is positive and uplifting; some of it is just the opposite.

Unless we purify our energy systems, kundalini can create major problems. Sometimes our blocks are so great, the kundalini can't even rise. In my practice, I devote a lot of time to helping clients clear out their old issues, examining everything from soul or past-life issues to current situations that they dislike, such as a hated job.

Energy cleansing involves clearing out more than our own old issues. I believe that up to 80 percent of our problems actually originate in others and that we have assumed these issues energetically. The most common origins of others' energies include our ancestry, family of origin, and peer group, but also every institution, religion, workplace, and group in which we have been involved. We absorb these energies through our energy field and store them inside our chakras. You cannot fix a problem that is not your own. You cannot heal someone else's physical illness, feel their feelings for them, or mend someone else's broken heart. It is important to gently release others' energy so that you can concentrate on your own issues. Ironically, being "only" yourself helps you become a better friend to others.

What you heal energetically will heal your body, mind, and soul. What you heal in your body will also shift you energetically, as well as affect your mind and soul. All purification techniques assist every part of you. In fact, anything you do with love will create more love—more health, better relationships, greater prosperity, and an enhanced kundalini experience.

The Yogi's Way to Cleanse

Every yogic practice recommends energetic exercises to prepare the body, mind, and soul for kundalini. The classic method is founded on the Eightfold Path of Yoga created by Patanjali in AD 200, which, in turn, has its origins in the Yoga Sutras of the Vedic path.

Purification includes many activities beyond breathing (prayanama) and postures (asanas). The following are a few, all of which will be explored in detail in part II:

- Bhandas (body locks)
- Mudras (gestures)
- Mantras (chanted words)
- Kriyas (exercise sets)
- Meditation techniques, including visualization and projection
- Regulation of the four basic instincts: food, sleep, sex, and self-preservation

Chapter 6 explores more yogic techniques for working with kundalini, and many of the practices described there will help foster a healthy kundalini awakening.

Ancient Idea, Modern Wisdom:
The Science of Kundalini Energy

Life is just a chance to grow a soul.

—A. Powell Davies

A long time ago, our ancestors believed in the power of knowing. This inner belief, supported by communal love, led to the observation of spiritual truths, including our unity with the Divine. It invited processes and medicines for healing and philosophies that formed the basis for good and productive lives. Centuries of war and violence shattered the eras emphasizing partnership and spirituality, however, forming a schism between science and spirituality.

There are now bridges across the chasm.

In times past, the science-minded among us have discounted the existence of an invisible energy such as kundalini because of its subtle nature. Times are changing. Science is now validating the benefits to kundalini-based practices and, going a step farther, even postulating reasons why kundalini just might exist.

Science has made major contributions to our cognitive understanding of ancient kundalini concepts. What happens biologically when the energetic serpent unwinds and rises to the crown chakra? What is suggested by the medical and other scientific communities? In this chapter, we're going to briefly touch on a few of the scientific areas explaining kundalini—namely, medical research—and theories behind kundalini effects. The concepts are introduced only briefly, just enough to give you a taste.

Medical Research and Kundalini

Why would the ancients spend years cultivating their kundalini? Why pass on spiritual tracts outlining methods of doing so? Why do so many contemporary wise women and men give their time to teach people to do so? Why do you—or might you—employ kundalini-based practices?

Medical research is starting to show what kundalini aficionados already know. Methods of cultivating the kundalini and working within its awakened glory leave us feeling better. Studies now reveal that the gains are widespread and include such practical benefits as stress reduction, anti-aging, addiction recovery, and even the healing of mental, emotional, and physical conditions.

One of the primary reasons for these physiological benefits is that all Indo-Tibetan practices necessitate breathwork for the safe activation of the kundalini. Clinical evidence now shows that yoga breathwork, called pranayama, effectively treats depression, anxiety, and post-traumatic stress disorders (PTSD), and it alleviates stress for victims of mass disasters. Kundalini-based yoga also improves asthma, diabetes, pain, and stress-related disorders, and it decreases blood pressure, heart rate, metabolism, and breathing rate. These effects in turn lead to lower anxiety and depression, healing of heart irregularities, decreased anger, treatment of insomnia, and even aid fertility. One research study showed that participants employing kundalini yoga techniques enjoyed a 58 percent reduction in muscle stress. And according to a study at Columbia University, kundalini-related practices, including meditation, diet, and yoga exercises, also serve as an anti-aging campaign, as they improve anti-inflammatory responses and stress reduction, in addition to the antioxidant benefits of a better diet.[25]

Trying to kick a habit? A study in India showed that addicts using an array of yoga, meditation, and spiritual and mind-body techniques showed positive improvements in psychological and psychosocial areas, as summarized on self-report questionnaires.[26] Looking to feel better? Yet another study compared the effects of kundalini yoga versus two other meditation techniques for treating obsessive-compulsive disorders (OCD), the fourth most common psychiatric disorder. The group practicing kundalini yoga techniques showed significant improvement in their OCD behaviors. The same practices are being effectively applied to relieve phobias, addictive and substance abuse disorders, major depressive disorders, dyslexia, grief, insomnia, and other sleep disorders.[27]

These results make common sense. When we're tense, we become stressed. We know what it's like to come home from work completely wiped out. Sometimes it takes all night to recover from our day—and years to recover from a string of hard days. Every issue is stored in our chakras. At any given time, we carry around more than a few days' worth of challenges. Our lifetime is locked within our bodies, our chakras holding blocked memories and energy we're finished with but have not yet released. Quite simply, it's almost impossible to get to the "old stuff" without a supercharged energy like kundalini to unblock and unlock it.

That's the easy explanation for the healing effects of kundalini. A bit more complicated, but more scientific, are the current theories presented by science. As you read through them in the next section, think about the fact that all of them are happening inside of your own body. When you do, kundalini becomes so much more than simply energy; it is the comet that lights the universe of *you*.

Theories Behind Kundalini's Effectiveness

Spiritual practitioners and teachers have touted many theories about the physiological mechanics of kundalini. Let's sidestep into a few of these and see what they might mean for you.

Quantum

Is kundalini part of a cosmological system? If so, this might account for some of its effects.

In quantum theory, everything is connected to everything else. The Vedas and Upanishads concur that there is only one consciousness, the entity called Brahman, underlying all of physical reality. Brahman created—and remains—everywhere at once. This means that we are intimately linked to both the Creator and the ongoing creation.

Physicists are realizing that this is the case in the "real world" as well. Evidence shows that the stars, blades of grass, thoughts, the beating human heart, and the dust of the cosmos are interconnected. In her book *The Field*, Lynne McTaggart outlines scientific evidence that reveals a subtle field of energy that surrounds everything. She calls it the zero-point field, or field of light. This field stores everything we are not using until we need it again.

This zero-point field is the equivalent of *maya*, the illusion of the physical world emanated from the Absolute. We are made of maya, as is everything around us, but we are so much more than maya as well. Mani Bhaumik, a fellow in the American Physical Society and the Institute of Electrical and Electronics Engineers, asserts that this unified field and the Brahman consciousness might be identical.[28] This knowledge means that kundalini-based practices really can result in their stated goal: an awakening to the truth of our unified state. Even on our hardest days, when lost in loneliness, we are already interconnected. We are already part of the greater creation. Kundalini helps us sear through the veil of separateness and wake up.

Electrical

Many theorize that kundalini is an electrical energy. Raise the electrical functions, and you improve the energizing and connectivity of the cells, organs, and nerves, also "upping the amp" on our magnetic fields.

Electromagnetism is light. Spiritualists continually insist that we are made of light; kundalini practitioners promise a return to light after climbing the ladder of the chakras. Research is now showing we actually *are* made of light. In fact, the body itself is a biophoton machine, and our DNA is a storehouse of light, which emits these small units of light.[29]

The truth is that in seeking enlightenment, we are simply activating all the light within us. We do not erase the lower frequencies of the lower chakras or physical organs, we simply transcend them, releasing the blocks and retaining the wisdom. The rising of the kundalini is essentially a return to our highest frequency of light.

Biomechanical

Kundalini practices are often performed by the body and can therefore reshape the body mechanically. Many of the benefits of yoga are incurred because it gets us moving—and moving the right way, realigning our skeleton and muscles. When the body is looser, the bodily fluids flow better, and we regain or achieve a higher state of physical health.

There's other research, however, that probes deeper into the body to see what kundalini is really doing. This theory, called the Movement Theory, was formulated by Itzhak Bentov, a progressive scientist. Bentov detected and recorded small bodily movements that occurred when subjects were meditating. These micromotions, as he called them, increased when breathing diminished and meditative awareness increased. He discovered that these motions in the body began with a standing wave in the aorta, the largest artery of the body. A standing wave forms when a wave is confined by boundaries or when two waves going different directions get together anyway.

The aorta travels along the spine to the floor of the abdomen and then, finally, into the pelvis, at which point it subdivides and continues down the legs. Bentov showed that at a certain point, a meditator's heart rate, respiratory rate, and descent of the diaphragm interrelate to create this aortic motion. The entire body, even the skull, starts to move in the same rhythm, producing magnetic fields above the head. Once this happens, the person can experience the kundalini reflex, the set of complex and sometimes uncomfortable sensations reported with kundalini activation, from tingling to experiences of bliss.

At some point, the brain begins to circulate an electrical current in both hemispheres, creating two pulsing magnetic fields of opposing polarities around the head. These pulse in harmony with the surrounding world. Essentially, the meditator has now formed an energetic antenna above his or her head that integrates into the geomagnetic force field of the earth, the electromagnetic and other energies of the solar system, and the universe at large. "Tuned in" above and below, the enlightened one is automatically aware of cosmic (and earthly) changes and adjusts effortlessly. This universally coherent state leads to the enviable healthiness and heightened conscious states noted in the yogi.

Dr. Swami Karmananda Saraswati, who writes about Bentov's work, suggests that kundalini, as the state of super-consciousness, is really a magnetic and bioelectrical attunement with the universe.[30] That means that our bodies are actually instruments for tuning in to the universe. Kundalini awakens us to this reality.

Hormonal

Many practitioners, including me, profess that the chakras lock into endocrine glands, affecting our hormone activities. Kundalini energy is called a fire, the serpent fire that ignites. What does it ignite but our hormones? And it is, in turn, lit by them.

A cycle called the metamorphic hormone cycle is implicated in the process of kundalini. As shared by Helen Fisher, who wrote *The Anatomy of Love*, testosterone might be the most active agent during infatuation, because it is implicated with certain other hormones that trigger sequentially until finishing with oxytocin and vasopressin, hormones that cause calm and peace. The initial punch of testosterone during an activation of kundalini might account for the reported increase in sexual feelings and, with the hormonal sequence concluding, the eventual shift to personal bliss.[31]

Every endocrine gland is important, but three of them are worth noting for their specific associations with the kundalini. As we know, kundalini energy rises from the base of the spine, from the first chakra, called the *muladhara* in Sanskrit. A glandlike body is actually located in the coccygeal body at the base of the coccyx. Composed of smooth muscle that can pulsate like an ejaculation, this body lies between the rectal wall and the tip of the tailbone. This area is fed by several nerves, arteries, and veins, and it directly influences the nervous system through chemical messages via the blood. It interconnects hormonal, circulatory, sympathetic, parasympathetic, and immune systems, and may very well be a key to metamorphosis. During excitation, such as during sex, the body produces nitric oxide and other neurotransmitters. Researcher Jane Dixon proposes that during maximum nerve activity, the spine is also supercharged with glutamate, calcium, and other ions, in addition to nitric oxide; this combination sets off a chain of reactions that causes sensations such as heat, tingling, and pressure to rise up the spine between the two sympathetic trunks, transmitted in a double-helix fashion.[32] The sympathetic trunks are two long nerve strands that run on either side of the spine, between the coccyx and the skull. This placement fits the classical kundalini description of the kundalini ladder.

As the kundalini climbs, it eventually makes its way to our heart. This "stopoff" is more critical than we might think. The heart is the major endocrine gland of the body, and its electrical field is sixty times greater in amplitude than is our brain's. Its magnetic field is 5,000 times greater.[33]

When we're under stress, our heart loses coherence, or the ability to achieve balance and harmony between all parts of our being. The heart perceives stress holistically, however. Critical thoughts, a pessimistic attitude, or even spiritual misperceptions can throw off our heart and create a downslide on our mental, emotional, and physical health. Conversely, by accentuating high-hearted ideals such as love, hope, and truth—those reinforced by the yogic principles explored in chapter 8—we enjoy an immediate and long-term improvement in our physical, relational, and mental health and general well-being, as proven through research by the Institute of HeartMath.[34]

Over time, our rising kundalini climbs into the higher spiritual glands. The ultimate goal is the crown chakra, or *sahasrara*, often called "the mystical gland." Here, Shakti merges with Shiva—the female with the male, the body with the spirit—and enlightenment ensues. Their exact meeting place is the brain's pineal gland. Physiologically, the pineal gland is located near the center of the brain on the left side of our brow. It contains the same rods and cones as are present in our eyes, underscoring the esoteric idea that it is the center of prophecy. It also secretes hormones vital to our health, including melatonin, which induces sleep, and serotonin, which makes us happy. These two hormones have also been implicated in our ability to attain states of higher consciousness, even while sleeping.

The pineal gland also formulates dimethyltryptamine, or DMT, one of several "spirit molecules" that appear to initiate alternative states of consciousness, hallucinations, and visions.[35] Another pineal-produced neurochemical, called pinoline, triggers psi-experiences such as psychic visions and spiritual contacts.[36]

Enlightenment doesn't sound so mystical when we read a list of brain chemicals and hormones, but it is important to remember that the chemicals are a result, not a cause, of our careful work to coax Shakti to meet Shiva.

Spine and Central Nervous System

The chakras are tied to the spine, or nervous plexus areas. The rising of the kundalini through the chakras improves central nervous system functioning but also changes the way our brain operates. Specifically, the brains of experienced Tibetan Buddhist meditators, after meditating, showed significant alterations in the cingulate gyrus, a ridge in the medial part of the brain; several parts of the prefrontal cortex and cortex; the parietal lobe; and the thalamus. These brain areas affect emotions, aggression, mental acuity, creativity, memory, speech, and orientation—all skills needed for successful social functioning.[37]

Additional studies have shown changes in brain waves due to kundalini practices. For instance, one test revealed that kundalini yoga breathing increased alpha wave activity during meditation.[38] The alpha wave is usually induced with relaxation and the closing of the eyes, and encourages the advancement of meditation, telepathy, intuitive awareness, and the spiritual states of consciousness.[39] Yet another study, this one employing Tantric yoga meditation, demonstrated an increase in alpha and theta frequencies among proficient meditators. The autonomic nervous system reactions spiked when the meditators approached the yogic ecstatic state of intense concentration.[40] Theta brain-wave frequencies are the gateway to higher states of consciousness and are linked to extraordinary states of consciousness such as trance, self-hypnosis, subliminal superlearning, astral and time travel, lucid dreaming, channeling, and clairvoyance.[41]

What might these revelations mean for us? Kundalini heals and benefits our autonomic nervous system. Over time, we don't have to consciously think about healing ourselves. Instead, our body and its functions becomes more fluid and caring for itself. The "upsizing" in brain waves is equivalent to the beginning of enlightenment, the ability to operate on a higher level. Many kundalini systems adhere to the notion that the higher an individual evolves, the more likely one is to develop siddhi, or extraordinary gifts. These studies seem to suggest that possibility.

Living with the Serpent
✳
Kundalini in
the Divine Life

part II

Kundalini Practices

The youth gets together his materials to build a bridge to the moon, or, perchance, a palace or temple on the earth, and, at length, the middle-aged man concludes to build a woodshed with them.

—Henry David Thoreau

The reality of everyday life makes it especially important to engage our kundalini. How else are we to get enough energy to maintain our busy lives—and enjoy them? Kundalini is an energy, and this means it is critical to find kundalini practices that connect us with this engaging energy.

There are many different approaches to kundalini energy and the philosophy of how to work with it. Though there are hundreds of processes for the management of kundalini, inevitably you will enter a discipline through one of these two paths: Vedic and Tantric philosophies. (The Vedanta, discussed in chapter 1, could be seen as a triplet to the other two, or else a part of the Vedic.) From here, you will be directed to various yoga practices.

chapter six

All yoga practices, no matter what they are called, begin and end with an understanding of kundalini, the basic energy of life.[42] To access kundalini is to do yoga; to be a student of any form of yoga is to touch your kundalini. For this reason, this chapter delves into the path of yoga—not the different practices themselves, but the ideas taught by yogis. This chapter features a few of the different yoga practices that can increase your kundalini power in real life. We'll cover the use of pranayama (deep breathing and release), meditation, mantras (chants and affirmations), asanas (movements and postures), mudras (gestures), visualization, and bhandas (body locks). Every technique is beneficial for cultivating a kundalini awakening, for helping you as experience rising kundalini, and for helping you integrate the lessons and gifts that stem from kundalini activation.

Know that there are thousands of books, Internet sites, classes, and teachers that can help you develop or further your understanding of and work with kundalini. Remember that it's important that you customize your own practice and keep doing so. As the kundalini rises within, it changes you. As you change, so does your relationship with the kundalini and, ultimately, the Divine. To live the light of your own divinity is to keep transforming the path to your divinity. The approaches in this chapter can get you going, supplement an intermediate to advanced practice, or simply assist you in stress reduction. Above all, enjoy the practices and techniques you undertake, as the kundalini is ultimately a door-opener to joy.

Also know that you do not have to use an Eastern discipline to work with your kundalini energy. Exploring kundalini on your own through therapeutic means, by performing tai chi or qi gong, or through a major religion, including Islam, Judaism, or Christianity, will invoke the same basic concepts and even require similar practices. (Chapter 12 explores the spirituality of kundalini in more detail.)

Pranayama:
The Kundalini Breaths

We breathe from the moment we are born, but most of us have little regard for this act or its importance—until we are short of breath, anyway. Breathing is one of the most vital tools for climbing the ladder to our enlightenment, and kundalini practices are always intertwined with conscious breathing. Pranayama is deep breathing that enables the activation and rising of the kundalini. Most yogis agree that breathing is essential for a safe kundalini awakening. One particularly effective breathing process is taught in kriya yoga, a kundalini-based practice easily integrated into everyday life.

The word *kriya* in Sanskrit means "action, deed, or effort." Most practitioners incorporate various kriyas into their normal lives. Kriya yoga is an important process for activating kundalini, only recently emerging into the public eye. Favored by Paramahansa Yogananda, author of *Autobiography of a Yogi*, kriya yoga helped open the Western world to the importance of yoga during the twentieth century. Based on the principles of karma yoga, as well as certain other forms of Tantric and kundalini yoga, kriya yoga asserts that the indwelling soul, or *ya*, should be enabled to regulate all our actions, or *kris*. The cognate *kri* is also the root of the word *karma*. Whereas karma, the principle of cause and effect, refers to action, *kri* means "to do." Kriya yoga is, therefore, the union with the Infinite through specific actions.[43]

The purpose of conducting kriya yoga rites is to become more sensitive to your indwelling soul. The core of kriya yoga is conscious breathing—a breathing that not only fills your body, but also your soul. Upon becoming "filled," your soul can assert authority over your mind and eventually liberate itself from your body, ultimately achieving the state of samadhi, or realization of the Absolute.[44] Meanwhile, the kriya practitioner lives the life of service, giving of self to assist others.

Why not see how even the simplicity of breathing can transform *your* life?

Kriya Breathing

This exercise is adapted from one on the Spiritual Path of Yoga website by Furio Sclano, a minister with the kriya yoga–based Center for Spiritual Awareness.

- Sit on an armless chair and inhale for ten seconds. Now do the following:
- Hold your breath for ten seconds, and then exhale with a double exhalation, also for ten seconds. (A double exhalation involves breathing out, then pausing, then breathing out again. It sounds like "huh huhhhhhhh.")
- Repeat five or six times.
- Close your eyes and focus on the point between your eyebrows.
- Connect with the Divine (as you understand the Divine).
- Simply watch your breath. Do not try to control or change it.
- When inhaling, repeat this word in your mind: *hong*.
- When exhaling, repeat the word *so*, pronounced as "saw," in your mind. *Hong-so* is Sanskrit for "I am he."
- Practice this *hong-so* inhalation/exhalation for ten minutes.
- Now stop concentrating on your breathing and focus again on the point between your eyebrows. Stop thinking.
- Become aware of light and only light. Gaze into this light and release yourself to the Divine.
- Gradually end your session and resume your daily activities.[45]

Meditation Made Marvelous

Meditation is one of the most important activities you can do to work with your kundalini. As shared by Tantric and chakra expert Harish Johari, meditation alone cannot arouse a kundalini activation, which makes it safe for those scared of activating the kundalini unexpectedly.[46] Using meditation to help your kundalini process makes you impervious to a "kundalini attack."

There are many types of meditation that use postures, bhandas, breathing techniques, visualizations, chanting, silence, and even walking or talking. No matter the form, meditation can be explained in a simple definition: *meditation is a way of awakening.*

For many of us, meditating is not easy. It's hard to concentrate, the most important aspect of meditation. It's also difficult to find the time and a quiet setting. So don't try—just *do.* Simply become aware of your breath throughout your everyday life. This helps you focus and increase your ability to be at one with yourself and others. Other processes and techniques can be added, but all meditation starts with breathing, which is something you do all the time anyway.

Breathe into the moment. Breathe into the words you speak. Breathe into a project or the opening of your palm or the aroma of fresh bread. The word for "breath" and "spirit" are the same in many religions. All breathing is a spiritual experience. *Breathe.*

A few other tips, important for both the beginner and the advanced meditator, include:

Keep it simple—and the same: Employ the same process at the same time every day and in the same place, if possible. If you use tools, use the same ones as often as possible. Rituals ease your mind and body.

Bend and stretch: Be comfortable before you settle. The asanas, or physical postures, of yoga were specifically designed to help the body prepare for sitting in meditation. So if you practice physical yoga, consider doing some simple postures before finding your meditation position.

Occupy your body: You live in your body. Breathe into the fullness of it and visit every corner of it.

Wander awhile: The best way to keep your mind from wandering is to give it permission to do so. Let it play before you give it time off from thinking.

Breathe: Use any breathing technique you like or simply breathe. If your mind forgets it's on vacation, concentrate on your breath.

Chakra-Based Meditation

One helpful way to meditate is to use a chakra-based approach. By "going chakra," we can:

Boost our most essential chakras: We all have chakras that serve more vital purposes for us than others. If we're an opera singer, for instance, our fifth chakra is innately stronger than the others. If we're a football player, we employ our physically adept first chakra for most endeavors. Each chakra is best strengthened with certain types of meditations rather than others. By selecting the meditation style that supports the chakras most active in our lives, we enhance our strongest qualities.

Heal a block: Our kundalini gets stuck in chakras that are blocked. By meditating in or through the inhibition, we can potentially heal the issue and encourage our kundalini to climb. (See the exercise "Easing Kundalini-Triggered Chakra Symptoms" in the meditation section of this chapter for a step-by-step method.)

Develop an underdeveloped chakra: When we focus on a weaker chakra, we awaken the qualities latent in that chakra and promote a new way of interfacing with the world and our kundalini.

In short, a chakra-based approach develops our gifts, mitigates the effects of the kundalini, clears blocks, alleviates concerns, develops our weaker qualities, "lets off the steam," and helps us work through triggered issues.

Conducting a chakra meditation is no different than performing any other meditation. It starts and ends with breathing, and there's a lot of relaxing and mind release in between. If centering on a certain chakra, however, you can supplement the process with chakra-based tools and activities, which are shared in chapter 2. For instance, you can put your hands on the related body part; wear, surround yourself with, or envision the chakra color; or concentrate on a chakra's attribute or theme (see chapter 2 for a listing of these). You can also sound the seed syllable encoded in a chakra center; focus on a number, symbol, or picture associated with the chakra; or hold a chakra-related gemstone (see the following chart for some examples).

	Chakra 1	Chakra 2	Chakra 3	Chakra 4	Chakra 5	Chakra 6	Chakra 7
Seed syllable	LAM (pronounced "lum")	VAM (pronounced "yum")	RAM (pronounced "rum")	YAM (pronounced "yum")	HAM (pronounced "hum")	AUM/OM (pronounced with a long O)	None
Meaning	Renewal	Pairing	Creation	Balance	Direction	Choices	Spiritual light
Picture	Serpent, transformation	Fish, flow	Bird, freedom	Mammals, connection	Celestials, guidance	Angel, heaven-earth relationship	Rainbow, divine reflection
Gemstones	Ruby, garnet, bloodstone	Moonstone, carnelian	Citrine, sunstone	Rose quartz, emerald	Blue topaz, turquoise	Purple fluorite, amethyst	Diamond, clear quartz

Here are a few meditative approaches that work with the various chakras. These suggestions employ my twelve-chakra system.

First chakra: Highly physical, this chakra responds to postures, mudras, and meditations conducted while moving, such as walking or running, or when standing. Make sure your feet are on the floor. Postures can be aerobically oriented. If this is one of your strongest chakras, try challenging yourself to become more and more successful at your meditation.

Second chakra: Meditate near water. If using asanas, employ those that emphasize waterlike grace and fluidity. Use visualizations that employ the full five senses. Pay attention to what you are wearing, as this chakra is sensually based. When meditating, pay special attention to the feelings in your body.

Third chakra: This chakra responds to organization, detail, and thought. Try structured, breath-based meditations that progress in difficulty over time. Asanas should be practiced in a series. Consider using affirmations and meditations that clear the mind, as people with dominant third chakras can tend toward worrying. Meditate at the same time and place each day.

Fourth chakra: This chakra affirms love, healing, and relationships. Meditate holding an image of a loved one or the Divine, or with a partner guiding or sitting with you. Do postures or chanting as a couple. Imagine beams of light interconnecting you with loved ones.

Fifth chakra: Chanting, mantras, or listening to music can be ideal meditative techniques, as is prayerful communication with spiritual guides or the Divine. Even reading poetry or inspirational writing can be meditative for this chakra.

Sixth chakra: Use visualizations and guided meditation; surround yourself in a setting that is visually pleasing. Use colors that reflect the meditation. You can also use *yantras*, symbols or designs that have meaning. There are yantras with agreed-upon purposes, used by various yogis and practitioners; you can see many on the Internet. You can also develop your own personal yantra, or picture images.

Seventh chakra: Concentrate on white light. Some people fast before a deep seventh-chakra meditation. Development of this chakra should not be rushed or pushed. This is the final in-body chakra, the home of the divine masculine energy. Here, the feminine kundalini merges and blends into the divine light of the masculine— and this process can take time. To speed through it is to miss the delight, but it can also cause us to skip some of the important integration process and become too "high" or spacey.

Eighth chakra: The goal of this chakra is neutrality and awareness of service. Meditation can involve the safe use of remote viewing, astral travel, regressions, and shamanic protocol. The protocol called karma yoga could be useful.

Ninth chakra: This chakra is oriented toward service, promoting global harmony and love amongst all beings, sentient or not. When meditating, focus on higher principles and figures of light that have made a difference in this world.

Tenth chakra: Employ sounds and visualizations from nature. Conduct your meditation in as natural a setting as possible, sitting or standing as close to the earth as you can. Consider walking meditations in nature and using natural elements as a focus. Make sure you ground into the earth, perceiving yourself as a tree with deep roots and branches that lead to the sky.

Eleventh chakra: Set goals before the meditation and consider using meditation as a way to become aware of supernatural forces inside and around you, becoming one with the guidance that can teach you to direct these forces ethically. Attune to moving natural forces, such as wind, waves of the sea, and the sweeping of the sand to create changes within you or to bring you messages.

Twelfth chakra: Completely empty yourself of any goals or purpose for a meditation except to open to the mystery and in-the-moment magic of the Divine. Seek yourself within the Divine, and the Divine will find you.

Ready to design your own chakra meditation? First, prepare for your meditation by considering the following details:

- Select a site for meditating based on the chakra you most want to connect with.
- Choose a position—for instance, sitting, standing, walking, running, posing, or employing a posture.
- Decide if you are going to use a partner or not.
- Select implements, such as a gemstone.
- Decide what to wear.
- If desired, choose focus points, such as a place in the body, a symbol, number, sound, or theme.

When you're ready to meditate, do the following:

In a comfortable position, breathe deeply, holding any implement you have chosen to help you ground your energy. As you relax, bring your focus to the chakra on which you are concentrating. The spirit of your breath gently opens this energy center on every level, and you resonate with it, settling into the myriad sounds, shapes, colors, and gifts it has for you. You completely erase all goals except for being the "you" that you are in this special space.

After a time, you notice that this chakra is now shining and glowing. Through it, the Divine now gives you a message. You lovingly accept this insight, allowing it to illuminate your entire being. When you feel complete, shift your focus from the chakra to your heart and breathe deeply until you are ready to rejoin the conscious world. The kundalini, at whatever level it has been flowing, settles into a level that is safe and comfortable for your everyday existence, and you awaken to your everyday self.

Easing Kundalini-Triggered Chakra Symptoms

This is a simple meditation for working with energetic blocks within a chakra affected by kundalini activation.

1. Breathe deeply, drawing your breath from your abdomen.
2. Ask the Divine to accompany and guide you through this exercise.
3. Invite the earth to sustain and heal you through this process.
4. Now focus on the symptom creating a disturbance.
5. Track this energy to its chakra of origin.
6. Gradually make your way to the outer ring of that chakra. Breathe deeply into it, and allow yourself to surrender to an image, memory, sense, feeling, sound, or another intuitive communiqué that explains the origin of this block.
7. Once you feel like you understand this issue, ask the Divine to guide you into the inner circle of this chakra, the place of spirit within.
8. From this place, ask to understand the reasons you experienced the trauma or misperception held in the

chakra's outer ring. Then ask to receive the gift available from that experience.

9. Forgive yourself or others for the challenge that brought this teaching, and ask the Divine to lift the symptoms that have been affecting you.

10. Embrace the gift, take a few breaths, and return to your normal state of consciousness.

Guided Visualization

Guided visualization is meditation that uses the imagination to create changes in your psyche, especially important to the Tantric and Vedantic traditions. As compared to the classical Vedic track, which emphasizes the release of the soul from bodily concerns, these two pathways highlight the integration of the body with the soul. Sensual experiences are considered bridges between the physical and the spiritual. Guided visualization is one such tool for employing the senses, employing pictorial imaging to generate changes in the psyche. The key to visualization is to become part of the picture while employing all your senses, so you create and enjoy a full experience and, in doing so, unblock the pathway for the kundalini to climb.

Visualization can also help us clarify choices, solve problems, receive messages, open to revelation, gain a better understanding of a person or situation, perform healing, and even glimpse parts of the future. Most individuals visualize through the sixth chakra, the energy center imbued with the gift of clairvoyance, or clear seeing. When I teach visualization, I help individuals open this energy center, but I also emphasize the seventh chakra. Housed in the pineal gland, the seventh chakra gathers different information than does the sixth and shares it in an unusual way.

These are the visualization processes embedded in the sixth and seventh chakras:

The sixth chakra: Based in the pituitary gland, this chakra is the most well-known center for visualization. The center of clairvoyance, the pituitary gland is divided into two physical sections, front and back, each of which performs a different psychic task.

The posterior pituitary gathers information from our unconscious and the Divine. This data streams into the backside of our sixth chakra and is evaluated and interpreted based on our self-image. If we like ourselves, we will perceive the highest possible choices. If we don't, our unconscious will automatically eliminate optimum choices and keep the most challenging ones. We select our favored option and project this decision through the front side of the pituitary gland. The projected energy manifests our reality.

Our pituitary gland presents us with this information in visual mediums, translating messages into images, colors, shapes, motion-picture shows, and still shots—everything and anything pictorial. If your visualizations are colorful and photographic, you are using your sixth chakra.

The seventh chakra: Did you know you can receive images through your pineal gland? Compared to colorful sixth-chakra visions, the seventh-chakra pictures come only in black, white, and the shades in between. This is because the pineal gland reflects levels of consciousness and purity of spirit.

We view through the pineal gland to assess integrity, truth, and honesty. White signifies purity and a high degree of spiritual veracity. Black could mean the opposite, as in representing dishonesty or lack of truthfulness, but it might also indicate a lower stage of development or a state of denial. White does not always mean good, and black does not always mean bad. The two extremes simply point out an adherence to divine will versus a "timeout," or resistance to higher will. The continuum of gray illustrates the grades and stages in between.

Imagine I am evaluating a prospective job. A brilliant white would confirm that the job enhances my spiritual destiny. It does not mean I will like the job or even get it, only that it suits me at the highest possible level. If I envision black, the job is not supportive of my true self, or there is more to be revealed. Gray would suggest that this job is mixed in terms of its suitability.

It is helpful to tap into both the pituitary and the pineal glands when using guided meditations or visualizations. We are then provided a full-color, three-dimensional picture screen, as well as a spiritual assessment. The following guided meditation can help you learn how to access the viewing powers of both chakra centers.

EXERCISE

The Path in the Pituitary and Pineal: *Visualizing Truth*

To visualize through your sixth chakra is to see through a prism. The world is full of rainbow colors, which form literal or metaphysical messages. To look through the lens of your seventh chakra is to assess your images for awareness, to ascertain how much of the Divine is in a situation. To blend both is to perceive truth.

Select a topic and create a question from it. Now sink into a relaxed, meditative state. Feel the support of the earth underneath you and the illumination from the heavens above. Know that you are safe and supported as you bring your attention to the space just above your nose. Breathe into this area, relaxing your body.

Bring your awareness into the sacred space in the middle of your pituitary gland, which is behind the base of your nose, in between your eyebrows, in the center of your brain. This area glows with an iridescent lavender light, in which you bask. Your cares begin to drift away; you cannot even remember them. You remember only the question you desire to ask your higher self and the Divine.

The beautiful light surrounding you begins to change. Colors emerge and shift into myriad forms, literal or metaphysical. These transform into an entirely different world, with you in the center of it.

On your left side is a brilliantly lit door. This is the gateway into your pineal gland. You open this door, and the brightest white light you have ever imagined streams into the room. It is warm and cool at the same time, objective and loving simultaneously. Again, focus on your question. The colors and light around you morph again, this time creating an image or set of pictures, which are now various shades of black to white.

You obtain the answer that you need from the emerging visualizations, which seem to have a life of their own. If you require an interpretation, ask the Divine to send you more images. Ask for insight until you feel complete.

Now ease your focus over to your heart and breathe deeply. The images in your mind fade, but you are left with an instilled sense of peace and serenity. You know the answer to your question. Breathing back into your everyday reality, open your eyes when you're ready and adapt safely to the world around you.

The Melody of a Mantra

Mantras are chants or affirmations often used in meditation to open the self to sacred energy. Often called "sound symbols," they invoke spiritual forces and may also be represented in a visual form.

Nearly every religion or spirituality makes use of mantras. A mantra is any process that invites a devotional practice; it can be a hymn or a chant, a repeated part of a sacred text, a poem, a prayer, a song, or even a magical incantation. It might be a name of a god or one of the names of God. A mantra helps you join with the Divine and embody its characteristics.

You can turn your own name into a mantra, or take a positive statement and, through focus, transform it into a mantra. Some people even use pictures representing the idea behind a mantra as a focal point. Anything that creates a worshipful attitude—including a behavior, feeling, idea, or statement of a goal—can be a mantra.

We are going to concentrate on verbal mantras, as the energetic effectiveness of a mantra is related to the eighty-four meridian points on the tongue and the mouth. Meridians are energy channels that run throughout the body and disperse chi (or qi), much in the same way the nadis circulate prana. (Some people believe these two-channel systems are one and the same.) Each of the major meridians is represented on the tongue as energetic points that link with the in-body channels. Different sounds operate like different codes, which unlock your higher spiritual centers.[47]

Yoga scripture frequently uses simple sounds, such as Aum or Om, So, Ah, and Hum. These Sanskrit sounds seem simple, but their power is incredible. In Sanskrit, each letter carries meaning, as do combinations of letters. Therefore, the smallest of words is a sacred energy, able to invoke a great spiritual force. For instance, chanting the chakra seed syllables mentioned earlier in this chapter can draw the kundalini to the representative chakra or heal an issue impeding the kundalini flow. I find that chanting two of the seed syllables together opens a passageway between chakras, forging an alliance that helps manifest a desire. As an example, you can link your first chakra, which governs security and money, with your heart chakra, which reflects healing and love, by chanting those chakras' seed syllables: Lam and Yam (pronounced "lum" and "yum"). This influential combination could attract an enjoyable job that could also pay your bills.

Know that you do not have to have a "good" voice to chant a mantra. Your voice is your own, as are the effects of a mantra.

I have designed two simple exercises using mantras for healing and well-being. The first exercise employs the Aum, which is said to incorporate the entire energy necessary to help the kundalini rise. Aum (or Om) represents the material and material aspects of the Absolute and can open you physically and spiritually.[48] It is probably the most popular sound for meditation, prayer, and songs.

The second mantra exercise will stretch your imagination. You will create your own mantra, one to accelerate, calm, soothe, smooth, love, motivate, and embrace your own kundalini process. This will be your personal kundalini mantra to use whenever and however you want.

EXERCISE

The Aum or Om Mantra

The Aum or Om is the most sacred symbol in Hinduism, representing Brahman, or the Absolute. This exercise will help you open to its powerful message.

Take a few moments and concentrate on the sound of Aum in your head. Savor the feel, texture, and shape of this intonation. Now bring the Aum into your heart, and feel its sweet sound vibrate. After your heart feels full, bring your Aum into the center of each chakra, one at a time, continuing to enjoy this sound silently. Finally, let the sound of Aum reverberate throughout the entirety of your body until it surrounds you and you are wrapped inside of it, a butterfly in the cocoon.

When you are ready, verbalize your Aum any way you want—fast or slow, low or high. Find your right speed, sound, or pitch, and sound this Aum through the entirety of your heart, back to front, and then throughout the totality of your body. Let yourself become the Aum.

Continue to sound Aum until you feel complete.

After breathing deeply, slowly return yourself to an awareness of your everyday reality.

The Aum or Om affirms the recognizable and nonrecognizable aspects of God. You can use this sound anytime you want during the day to gain a sense of peace, calm, and fulfillment.

Making Your Own Mantra

Many people believe that the most effective mantra is one that is personalized. You can create mantras for any reason. You might design a generic mantra, one designed to meet a specific goal or one that expresses your true essence. When carefully sculpted, a mantra works like a program in a computer, carrying out a desired effect.

Here is a process for creating a mantra for your kundalini process. You can use this process as a framework to devise any other desired mantra.

> *Compose yourself and breathe deeply. Your breath ushers in a state of peace and calm. With your mind floating and free, focus it on the idea of kundalini. Simply sense, without interpretation, everything that comes to you about kundalini; feel, smell, hear, see, acknowledge, taste, and be with the kundalini within you.*
>
> *Let your kundalini be wherever it is. Sense where it is in your body and energy system; let it be. Now invite it to share its own personal sound with you.*

This sound conveys the impression of the kundalini as it is right now, as well as what it will become. You might hear this sound; you might also put images, colors, shapes, textures, and impressions into the mix. When you are ready, invite this sound and its accompanying qualities into your chest and then upward into your throat. Begin to sound this mantra.

Stay with your personal kundalini sound or song as long as you feel like it. Commit it to memory, and return to it whenever you want.

Asanas:
Movements Toward Joy

Asanas are central to a yoga practice because of their physical, mental, emotional, and spiritual benefits. On the physical level, the movements, various postures and poses, are excellent for our health. There are sixty-six basic poses in classical systems such as hatha yoga, most of which provide stretching and toning. These types of postures work by first restricting a part of the body and, upon release of the posture, reoxygenating that same part. This process improves strength and stamina, aids in weight loss, and helps control blood pressure. It is well known that yoga reduces stress and aids flexibility of the body.

Certain yoga styles, including versions like power yoga and Iyengar yoga, go a little further and serve as aerobic exercise. Other practices, like Bikram yoga, add a cleansing component: Bikram is performed in heated rooms, which, along with the asanas, encourage the release of toxins via sweating. All yoga helps us release the feelings trapped in our bodies, and the philosophical principles of yoga promote mental health and actions consistent with our values.

The classic method of yoga is founded on the Eightfold Path of Yoga created by Patanjali in AD 200, which, in turn, has its origins in the Yoga Sutras. According to Patanjali, the asanas specifically represent the first limb of the Eightfold Path, which invites us to discover our own restrictions. If we can only bend to the right instead of the left, we can embrace our current level and, if possible, move beyond. Some people, however, question the pursuit of yoga because of their restrictions. I've watched many a client blush, embarrassed to share why they resist yoga. Some don't think they'll fit into the current "designer yoga fashions," while others are afraid they will look foolish. One woman simply pointed to her stomach and said, "This is in the way."

The first time I ever went to a yoga class, I was five months pregnant. As I proceeded with my pregnancy, I reached the point where I was fortunate if I could even stretch my arms and legs, and even then, I constantly toppled over. I loved going to yoga, though, if only for the few minutes of quiet it afforded me.

Don't get scared of the advanced yoga moves. You might already be employing them, or maybe you'll never choose to do more than stand and breathe. According to the Yoga Sutras, yoga is any position that is steady and comfortable. The goal of holding a particular position is to encourage concentration, discipline, and meditation, or connection with kundalini and the Divine. In other words, asanas assist in meeting many of the requirements of the Eightfold Path of Patanjali.[49]

To get the full benefits of the asanas, it is useful to learn them, especially complex ones, under the guidance of a teacher. What goals might you achieve? Asanas serve as terrific physical exercises, boosting health, the immune system, and well-being. Devotional asanas bond us body, mind, and soul, and the use of breathing, visualization, or other spiritual exercises through asanas help us connect with the Divine as well as our own intuition. Learning under the auspices of a guide ensures that we reap the full benefit of the practices while being safe. But to give you a taste of yoga asanas and their effects, here are two exercises. The first explains a basic yoga pose, one that is always good to learn and review. The second exercise is actually an approach to yoga, one that centers on chakra-based postures. As relayed earlier in the chapter, in our discussion about chakra-based meditation, customizing a kundalini practice to the chakras is useful in several regards. Different asanas support different chakras, as shown below.

EXERCISE

The Basic Yoga Pose

The mountain pose, as it is known in hatha yoga, is the most basic yoga pose and should be mastered before you advance to other poses. This standing pose will develop and strengthen your legs, improve your balance, align your hips and spine, and teach you to maintain equilibrium.

To practice it, stand with your feet together, hands at your sides, palms facing your legs. Relax your shoulders and keep your stomach tucked in, moving your chest and collarbone upward. Pretend you have a loop attached to your crown and a string tied to that loop. Someone above you pulls the string, and your entire spine and neck shift and stretch upwards. Breathing evenly through your nose, hold the pose for at least thirty seconds.[50]

EXERCISE

Chakra-Based Yoga

Kundalini requires a clear path through the nadis and chakras to make its way to the sacred space awaiting it in the seventh chakra. A chakra-based yoga practice employs classic yoga poses in order to cleanse, strengthen, and support each of the seven vital in-body chakras.

Following is a set of recommendations for setting up a chakra-based yoga practice.[51] Included is only a simple overview to acquaint you to the possibilities; you can look up specific yoga postures.

First-chakra yoga: In hatha yoga, the first chakra is supported with strengthening and standing asanas and those opening the pelvis. One example of this type of asana is the "bridge" pose, which strengthens and empowers us.

Second-chakra yoga: The "cobra" asana helps to stimulate the second chakra for our emotional well-being. For the second chakra, consider postures that move the synovial body fluids of the joints and stretch the connective tissue. These encourage flexibility and cleanse the body's fluids.

Third-chakra yoga: The "bow" pose helps us take our place in the world. Asanas that amplify and tone our core energy will warm the body and stimulate the mind.

Fourth-chakra yoga: The "camel" pose enables true love. The home of love, the fourth chakra responds to exercises that energize the heart and lungs, awakening our healing powers and feelings of interconnection.

Fifth-chakra yoga: The "fish" posture helps us absorb and communicate wisdom. Chanting is an ideal way to open this chakra, the center of our communication, and help us express ourselves.

Sixth-chakra yoga: The seated "yoga mudra" posture supports confidence in our life path. The sixth chakra, through which we access our inner vision, is the center of our self-image. The seated mudra irons out our misperceptions and "wrinkles" and helps us perceive our true and amazing self. Balancing poses bring balance to our total self, restoring hormonal, mental, and emotional integrity.

Seventh-chakra yoga: Meditation, especially after a yoga workout, connects our consciousness to that of the Divine.[52] Here, in this holy grail of divinity, we mingle the feminine kundalini with her masculine counterpart, unifying these two aspects of our personal self and our totality with the Divine.

Mudras

Thousands of years ago, yogis determined which areas on the hand represented different parts of the brain or body. These areas also mirror emotions and behaviors. A mudra is a hand position that opens the energy in the related hand area, sending a clear message to that part of the energy system. Kundalini yoga often employs mudras to help clear our chakras and nadis, which results in a smoother ride for the kundalini. Following are popular kundalini yoga mudras.

EXERCISE

Prayer Mudra

This mudra neutralizes or joins the right, masculine side of the body and the left, feminine side. It can be used for invocation, devotion, and centering.

To perform this mudra, bring your palms together in a classic prayer position in the center of your chest (at heart level). Press your hands together and gently hold the thumb knuckles at the center of the sternum.

EXERCISE

Gian Mudra

This mudra, designed to increase your wisdom and knowledge, is used with most meditative postures. There are two forms: passive and active. The first is receptive and calming, and the second projects energies.

> **Passive:** Put the tip of your thumb together with your index finger.
> **Active:** Curl your index finger under your thumb so your fingernail is against the joint of the thumb.[53]

Bhandas (Body Locks)

Bhandas are combinations of muscle contractions that alter nerve pressure, the flow of the spinal fluid, and blood circulation to direct the prana in the main energy channels. They assist in unlocking the granthi and clearing chakra blocks to make way for the rising kundalini, to raise consciousness, and to assist in healing.

In kundalini yoga, there are three main bhandas, which focus on the neck, diaphragm, and perineum, physical locations connected with the chakras housing the three granthi. This is why these bhandas are called body locks.

Following are brief descriptions of these locks. To activate them, ideally you should sit on your heels on the floor with your knees apart and facing at angles away from each other. Keep your back straight and your arms at your side. If this position is uncomfortable, sit in a straight-backed chair with your arms hanging at your side. (The diaphragm lock can also be done standing up, with your feet shoulder-length apart. While bending forward slightly, put your hands on your knees and keep your back straight.) All these locks should be done on an empty stomach. Beginners can do each repetition up to twenty-six times, with a minute in between each cycle. Please listen to your body, however, and only conduct as many cycles as you feel comfortable. I advise you to receive instruction if you have questions, or look for pictures on the Internet.

Root lock: (Sanskrit, *mul bandh*) Unites the prana and apana (upward and downward breaths), the key to the activation of the kundalini, mixing these two energies at the navel center. *Directions:* Exhale, then contract the anal muscle, drawing it in and up. Add a contraction similar to that felt in orgasm. Now draw your lower abdomen toward your spine, which pulls in your navel and draws your rectum and sexual organs upward. This body lock is usually applied at the end of a deep exhalation and released on the next inhalation. During the inhalation, sense energy moving up your spine and end the in-breath by focusing on your sixth or seventh chakras.

Diaphragm lock: (Sanskrit, *uddiyana bandh*) Opens the heart and invites prana through the sushumna into the neck, stimulating the hypothalamus, pituitary, and adrenal glands. This body lock is said to bring youthfulness. *Directions:* As you exhale, pull your upper abdomen muscles backward, toward your spine, and lift your diaphragm into your thorax. This lock is only safely applied on the exhalation.

Neck lock: (Sanskrit, *jalandhara bandh*) This lock activates secretions of the thyroid, parathyroid, and the pituitary glands. When powerful energy is rising, it often triggers your blocks. This body lock can help shift negative reactions. *Directions:* As you exhale, contract your neck and throat with your head level. Do not tilt your head forward. The prana can now travel more freely into your head.[54]

In addition to these three bhandas, there is a great lock, which applies the other three body locks simultaneously. We will cover the great lock in more detail in chapter 11, which discusses gender issues, as this lock relieves the preoccupation with sex, among other benefits.

Chakra Gemstones

Although using gemstones to work with kundalini is not a yoga-based practice, gemstones have been used for thousands of years to aid in healing, manifesting, and meditation focus. Following are a few of the hundreds of available gemstones, brief descriptions of their supportive qualities, and suggestions for which chakras from the twelve-chakra system each gemstone suits. (Chakra numbers are listed in parentheses.) The gemstones on this list can be used in conjunction with any meditation or other kundalini-based practice. For instance, you can hold a gemstone while meditating or visualizing, place it on the chakra affected by a kundalini rising, or carry it with you in order to heal a kundalini-triggered issue.

Gemstone	Activity
Agate, Fire	Boosts energy; clears safety and security issues (1)
Amethyst	Protects from negativity; aids in the healing of heart issues (4, 6)
Aquamarine	Enhances work and success; emotional balance (5)
Bloodstone	Aids in decision making; detoxifies (1)
Blue Topaz	Enhances peace and communication; heals throat issues (5)
Calcite	Cleanses blockages and digestive system (3)
Carnelian	Dispels boredom and apathy; alleviates emotional situations (2)
Celestite	Opens doorways to other dimensions (5, 9)

Gemstone	Activity
Chrome Diopsite	Transforms negativity; helps one become more mystical (8)
Citrine	Supports mental clarity; helps with digestive issues (2, 3)
Diamond, Herkimer	Invites global harmony; grounds the spirit into the body (9, 10)
Diamond, Pink	Promotes spiritual love; aids in healing heart issues (4)
Diamond, White	Empowers a spiritual commitment; helps heal brain issues (7, all)
Diamond, Yellow	Promotes positive thinking; helps heal digestive issues; opens a doorway to higher ideals (3, 9)
Emerald	Opens one to unconditional love; positively affects all physical illnesses (4)
Fluorite, Purple	Stone of discernment; integrates the two sides of our brain; eliminates falsity; invites harmony with one's true self (6)
Garnet, Grape	Assists in reaching goals; helps heal image issues (1, 6)
Garnet, Mandarin	Balances emotions; assists with creative projects, PMS, and prostrate and intestinal issues (2)

Gemstone	Activity
Garnet, Red	Attracts money and other primary needs; promotes healing in cases of potentially fatal illnesses and stress (1)
Garnet, Rhodolite	Enhances loving power; helps with heart issues (3, 4)
Granite	Provides grounding and connection to the earth and history (10)
Hematite	Grounds; releases mental constrictions; helps start new ventures (1, 10)
Iolite	Promotes subconscious healing; use for all problems (all chakras)
Jasper	Provides power and protection (10)
Lapis Lazuli	Enhances self-expression and connection to creative muses (5)
Moonstone	Enhances the feminine; soothes emotions (2)
Onyx	Opens spiritual powers; releases evil; grounds (8, 10)
Opal	Can do or help anything—pure light; I recommend opal for cancers of all types (12)

Gemstone	Activity
Pearl	Heals old wounds; helps in the healing of all major illnesses (1, 4, 8)
Peridot	Helps us express our real self; provides a connection to our spiritual self (4, 9, 12)
Quartz, Clear	Clarifies, purifies; can be programmed with other energies (7, 12)
Quartz, Pink or Rose	Heals love issues; adds playfulness; helpful for any issues of the heart and breasts (4, 11)
Quartz, Rutilated	Beneficial for healing and meditation; draws out negativity (2)
Quartz, Smoky	Promotes independence; purifies and detoxifies; provides grounding; dissolves blocks (1, 8)
Rubelite	Lifts low self-esteem; encourages forgiveness; energizes sluggish circulation (1, 3, 7)
Ruby	Invites wealth; activates life energy; supports ethical success; releases stress (1)
Sapphire, Blue	Enhances communication; addresses throat issues (5)
Sapphire, Pink	Enhances love; helps attract relationships (4)

Gemstone	Activity
Sapphire, Yellow	Enhances expanded thoughts; aids work success (3)
Spinel	Enhances achievement; beneficial for terminal illnesses and chronic stress (1)
Sugilite	Activates higher vision and mystical abilities and connections (6, 8)
Sunstone	Brings good fortune and relieves tension (3)
Tanzanite	Helps dreams manifest; helps one cope with transition; connects spiritual world (all chakras)
Tourmaline, Green	Integrates inner children; attracts abundance; alleviates all physical conditions (12)
Tourmaline, Pink	Balances relationships; helps us get our needs met (4, 11)
Tourmaline, Watermelon	Activates the heart; promotes interconnectivity; links us to our higher self (4, 11)
Turquoise	Promotes honest, full communication and opens us to higher guidance (5)

Ayurveda:
A Complete Life Program

One of the most comprehensive systems for ensuring a full life and healthy kundalini process is Ayurveda, a science for self-healing and self-realization. Ayurveda is actually a holistic medical system that encourages physical, emotional, mental, and spiritual health through a long list of approaches, including diet, herbs, exercise, and yoga regimes such as meditation and practices. The goal? To create harmony within our self, our higher self, and nature.

In his book *Yoga & Ayurveda*, David Frawley recommends the use of Ayurveda for ensuring a healthy and supportive kundalini experience. Kundalini is considered integral to the Ayurvedic process, which involves the enhancement and merging of three actual energies.

As we know, kundalini is the higher feminine energy that catalyzes our evolutionary potential. It is formed from an energy called *tejas*. Nectar, or *amrit*, descends from the crown chakra to feed the kundalini on its upward descent. This nectar, also called *ojas*, is a masculine spiritual energy that is purified through proper practices and development. This union creates the highest prana, the immortal life energy that the kundalini carries upward through the spine (see chapter 1). Called *buddhi*, this prana allows us to discriminate between the transcendent and the mortal and become who we really are.

To purify the ojas and thus nurture the upward-climbing kundalini, we employ a proper diet, tonic herbs, control of sexual energy, control of the senses, and devotion—all practices discussed throughout this book. The tejas is supported through controlled speech and other austerities (*tapas*), mantras, concentration exercises, and Jnana yoga, or the yoga of knowledge. We encourage our higher prana through pranayama, or breathing exercises; passive meditations emphasizing space and sound; and *raja,* or integral yoga. To become and remain balanced, we must simultaneously develop all three—ojas, tejas, and our higher prana. For instance, ojas will vitalize our life and help us mature. To increase the prana without the ojas is to become spacey, to lack grounding, and to possibly become deranged. To open only to the tejas (raw kundalini) is to burn ourselves up.[55]

Through Ayurveda, you personalize these concepts by determining your basic personality type, a combination of your *dosha* and *guna.*

A dosha is a cosmic force, the original ones being energy, light, and matter. These three original forces empower consciousness and determine specific constitutions, or mind-body types. Each of us is constructed of one force more than the others and can, therefore, be described as sharing similar biological traits with others in our type.

A guna could be described as a mental or spiritual state. Within our dosha type, we have the choice to operate at a higher rather than lower guna. Paying attention to everything from diet to mental activity helps us achieve a higher guna while we tend the practical day-to-day needs of our bodies.

The easiest path to becoming your true self is to follow the prescriptions for your dosha typology, decreasing the negative tendencies inherent in each and encouraging the highest and most spiritual qualities.

Nice to Meet You! What's Your Dosha?

Here is a brief description of the three doshas—called *vata, pitta,* and *kapha*—each of which relates to a central element and includes personality traits that can develop positively or negatively. Can you recognize yourself in these descriptions? With this knowledge, you can further pursue the path of Ayurveda to create a supportive plan to foster the rise of your kundalini.

> Vata: Relates to energy, the primal force of the universe, which actualizes through the element of air. Vata people are like air—action oriented, quick thinking, spirit based,

and always moving. The highest goal should be to move with divine will. To accomplish this, they carry strong healing gifts, are truly inspirational, and draw from a seemingly abundant source of vitality. If undeveloped, they can become easily distracted and superficial.

Pitta: Created from light, the instrument for seeking, knowing, and discerning. Light is the basis for the individuation of the soul, which means that the pitta person assists others with finding and following their soul paths. Light metabolizes in the material realm as fire. The fire and light qualities form intelligent and warm personalities. Most typically, a pitta person is perceptive, courageous, and a natural leader. When incomplete, they can become power hungry, subverting others to gain control. They can also be prone to anger and highly intolerant of others.

Kapha: Based in matter, the materializing of spirit and soul in form and substance. Elementally, kapha people relate to water, a nutrient that stabilizes, nourishes, and binds things together. They tend to exhibit the virtues of love, devotion, and faith, which serve them well, as they are life's comforters. Steadfast and balanced, they are loyal and nurturing. If undeveloped, kaphas shift into greed and materialism, eventually becoming owned by their possessions, rather than the other way around. When stuck, they can be really stuck, becoming inert and stagnating, sometimes turning to addictions to cope.[56]

There are specific activities that support each of these three basic types. For instance, vata people must pay special attention to their colon, as wind rules the colon. This bodily area energizes, and energizing is the main characteristic describing a vata person. Pitta people percolate, ripening thoughts, situations, and others to maturity. Biologically, pitta regulates digestion and transformation.

Imbalances appear through infection and inflammation; therefore, pitta people must tend the "fire systems" of their bodies. Kapha energy, on the other hand, serves through the power of cohesion. What "sticks us together" is mucus and phlegm. Kapha people must tend to the organs generating connectivity, love, and emotions, such as the stomach.[57]

All three energies interrelate within each of us. We cannot forget to feed our minds while working with our emotions and bodies. Further, we must care for not only each aspect of our physical body, but also our subtle or energy body and the causal—the energy we carry from lifetime to lifetime and experience to experience. Everything counts—as do we, even in this big world of ours.

How Do I Select a Practice?

Ultimately, living with kundalini is a dance. Kundalini tickles your fancy until you wake up and start a solo jig. It plays its music until you can't help but step in time with an important other. Its final goal is to engage you with the world, until pretty soon the entire universe is dancing with you.

However, there are so many approaches to kundalini that it can be overwhelming to know what to engage in. Should you practice yoga? If so, which kind? Should you attend classes, visit an ashram, or watch DVDs? Should you continue your current pursuit or start another altogether? Or should you give them all up and simply *be*?

Wherever you are in your decision making, the most important point is this: you are already dancing with your kundalini. If you are walking, breathing, thinking, loving, seeing, and being, your life force is generating within you. This powerful energy is already pulsing into and through your body. What remains are really two issues:

- Your degree of conscious interaction with your kundalini
- The needs of your daily life

Everyone wants to achieve a sense of oneness with the Divine, to enjoy a union with that special loved one, and to know oneself as worthy of love. This is what the kundalini path really offers. If you can gain that awareness by attending church, soaking in a hot tub, or practicing kung fu, that is what you must focus on. Most of us need a more mindful process, because most of us are frightened of our true divine nature, as well as our human needs. We are scared of our greatness. We are scared of our vulnerability. We are scared of opening to love, because we are scared that maybe we will discover we do not deserve love. To select any suitable kundalini practice—suitable because it meets our own criteria—is to open to the support needed to allay these fears and venture boldly into the spiritual unknown.

I cannot tell you what your particular criteria might be; no one can. I can, however, suggest a number of questions that can help you hone in on your needs, which, in turn, can help you select an appropriate practice. Ask yourself:

- What kind of money can I spend?
- What kind of time for a practice can I realistically build into my day?
- How can I balance my work, relationships, and personal needs to support a kundalini-based practice?
- What process will leave me feeling happier, more refreshed, calmer, and uplifted?
- What process will help me release stuck emotions, stress, and negative beliefs?
- What process will improve my self-esteem?
- What process will create a healthier body for me?
- What path will improve my connection to the Divine?
- Is there a path through which I can connect with my special "other" or my family or circle of friends?
- What path will I feel proud to tell my friends about?

- Which practice fits with my value system?
- Which practice will assist me in becoming the me I know that I really am?
- Which process feels safe at every level, including energetic and spiritual?
- Which path leaves me empowered?
- Which path makes me glow?
- What path do I think the Divine would want for me?
- When I look back at the end of my life, which path did I select?

These questions might lead you to where you already are or into yet another special place where you can dance with the cosmos and light your dreams.

My Own Kundalini Practices

Hercules was a famous Greek hero. One of his most notable endeavors was to wrestle and defeat a serpent when he was still an infant in the cradle. We can only imagine the strain and struggles involved in defeating a mighty and fearsome creature that would have been ten, fifteen, even fifty times longer than ourselves.

Many people read accounts of the kundalini and assume an equivalent effort in relation to taming the serpent energy. The task must be awful, hard, arduous. Certainly, one would have to concentrate hours each day to attain the objective. To let up would mean being struck with the fatal venom of this wild female.

We've explored some of the potential dangers of an uncontrolled kundalini, but the truth is that kundalini risings can also be gentle and sweet, or at least assuaged, especially if we are willing to face our issues with grace and honesty. Kundalini isn't out to get us. It is a form of our awakening consciousness, and because of this, it seeks to woo and assist us. It wants only to be awakened and allowed to court our divine enlightenment. If we're willing to cultivate our kundalini in small ways each day during our normal lives, it will reward us with kindness and assistance.

A few years ago, I began cultivating my kundalini in a more dedicated fashion, searching for short and simple ways to unfold it into my everyday life. I had little choice but to take this route—weeklong seminars in ashrams or three-hour yoga classes were not for me. As a single mother with two children, a foster daughter, and five animals, I couldn't plan dinner, much less a few kundalini moments. The best I could do was catch a few breaths when I could, sloppily achieve a few yoga poses in the morning, and eat a somewhat reasonable diet. I had a lot of excuses. I noticed, however, that these brief interludes of sanity had an effect: I felt better. I slept easier. I handled stress with more grace, and I tracked with my intuition more often. My spiritual guidance literally talked me through my days.

I have found that intuition is most beneficial when it gives me practical information. I wasn't receiving "grand advice," nothing like lottery numbers. Rather, a vision might remind me to turn on the oven so that dinner could bake. A trusted voice might announce it was time to get the car's oil changed. A dream even told me when to fly home to Minnesota from a business meeting in another state. Annoyed, I still heeded the dream's recommendation, staying away from home the extra night. The next day at the airport, I met the man whom I'm now dating.

After that experience, I perked up and began to integrate breathwork and meditation into my daily walks and so-called free time, which consists of sitting at schools, waiting to pick up kids, and the like.

One particular day, after I'd spent a few minutes drawing up my kundalini, I suddenly felt like reality broke down, or maybe I should say broke through. I sensed a group of amazing light, clear beings around me, full of kindness and wisdom. I also knew that the reality I was living in wasn't really "real." That reality was important but incomplete.

These beings insisted that they weren't in a separate reality. They weren't visiting from heaven, sitting light years or dimensions away and, from afar, flinging wisdom for humans to pick up and try to sort through. They were *here*. In fact, all of heaven is here; we simply can't perceive it. Their job, I was intuitively told, is to mirror the truth of this reality, the ultimate truth being that we are all connected through love. Because of their message, I began to call them the Spirits of Love.

I now sense and feel this web of love all the time, but not through the shimmering veil of separation. I can perceive this love in the eyes of a homeless person who smiles as I walk by and in my cat, who wakes me nightly to remind me of his existence. It's there in the guise of my sons, my clients, even myself at my most grumpy. Quantum theory insists that everything is connected and that, in fact, is in at least two places at once. Perhaps we are these Spirits of Love reaching through to remind ourselves of the same. If so, we must remember that we are on this earth to be on this earth. We don't need to cut chunks of time out of our lives to learn how to live our lives—we've only to open to the light that is already present to invite in more of it. Kundalini doesn't need to be wrestled to the ground to lift us to the skies.

Awakening by Transmission:
Bring On the Radiant Kundalini

The ground we walk on, the plants and creatures, the clouds above constantly dissolving into new formations—each gift of nature possessing its own radiant energy, bound together by cosmic harmony.

—Ruth Bernhard

Certain styles of yoga utilize transmission, or activation by a guru, to awaken kundalini. The student must then continue learning how to integrate the kundalini with his or her guru.

As a healer and teacher, I have frequently initiated clients and students to a kundalini awakening. I employ a process that is both gentle and loving; in fact, I consider it to be fail-safe because I'm not actually the one inciting the awakening. I consider transmission to be the territory of the Divine.

Let me introduce you to the process. Imagine yourself standing on a mountaintop, the same sacred site that has served as an altar of the Divine since time began. You might be anywhere in the world.

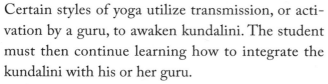

In fact, your personal mountain might be near a spring in the forest, an oasis in the desert, or atop a roof in a city. The Divine is everywhere you go; anywhere you are, the Divine is.

I now tap on your heart, asking the Divine to begin your kundalini initiation. Specifically, I request the kindling of the radiant kundalini, a third type of kundalini (after the feminine, red kundalini and the masculine, golden kundalini, discussed in chapter 2) that lies sleeping within the innermost sanctum of the heart chakra. When switched on, this radiant kundalini emanates from the center of each and all of the twelve chakras. As explained in chapter 2, the inner wheel of each chakra resonates with our true self and perfected spirit. This is the energy of enlightenment, the goal of kundalini-based systems. It beams spiritual brilliance throughout our body, mind, and soul. When awakened, it radiates outward from the center of the heart as a bright white light that shimmers and shines. Soon, this irradiant light awakens inside each chakra, inviting a full spirit embodiment.

This is the safest of the three kundalinis, the one that never harms, only heals—that never burns or scorches, only cools and assuages. Its presence will temper the potential harsh effects of both the red and golden kundalinis and ensure a sweet incorporation of both. It might also stop, delay, retract, or control the awakening or furthering of either of the other kundalinis, if that is for your highest good.

As soon as your heart's radiance quickens, I ask the Divine to ignite the radiant kundalini in your other chakras as well. After a moment or two, every one of your chakras begins to glow like a brilliant white star, and then, all at once, the sparkling energies merge, transforming you into a luminous star in your own right. You are now ready for the activation of your golden and red kundalinis.

I next ask the Divine to set your golden kundalini in motion or further its progress, if it's already been started. I summon the golden kundalini before the serpent, or red, kundalini, because the golden kundalini's spiritual nature will smooth and buffer the intensity of the red kundalini. The presence of the radiant kundalini guarantees a secure and smooth journey for the golden kundalini, while the golden kundalini promises a loving rising for the red kundalini.

Once the golden kundalini is thoroughly integrated, I then ask the Divine to rouse your red kundalini or further its climb if it's already in motion. Finally, I ask that the Divine carefully personalize the integration of these three kundalinis as time goes on. When all three kundalinis—red, golden, and radiant—are pulsing together, we are completely and harmonically balanced in every way. Our body can operate at its optimum. Our mind generates only wholesome and true thoughts, enabling clear decision making. Our soul can move toward intimacy and prosperity. And spirit reigns, transforming us into the enlightened sage we already are.

I have found that the key to a secure kundalini process is the awakening of the radiant kundalini, even if someone is in the throes of a tough feminine kundalini rising. No matter what, the radiant kundalini aligns our body with our spirit and the kundalini process with divine will.

Personally, this is the only transmission process that I ever use, mainly because I don't feel qualified to assess the hundreds of factors that determine a safe versus unsafe kundalini awakening. Even with the radiant kundalini in my toolbox, I am careful to assess the ethics of beginning an initiation or not. I almost always feel called to offer this process to people who are stuck in a negative kundalini spiral or just plain stuck in their lives. I often employ this process for students in my self-development classes, as they have already stated their interest in furthering their spiritual growth. I also teach this technique to healers who might find themselves in the position of initiating others or serving on the frontline of those in need of immediate kundalini care.

In all cases, I only perform transmissions for people who have a smart, savvy spiritual support system already in place—a system

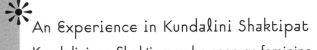

An Experience in Kundalini Shaktipat

Kundalini, as Shakti, may be seen as feminine electricity. If given a clear channel, its ascent is equivalent to turning on a light switch. If the wiring is faulty, we get jolted.

The key to a smooth initiation is love. Shaktipat is an initiation process that enables a loving awakening and ascent. It is often referred to as transmission because it occurs through a channel of love formed between the teacher and student, one in which the divine love of a teacher flows into the student. This unbounded love, transferred from the heart to another, creates a sense of deservedness in the initiate, who is now able to greet his or her feminine serpent kundalini with delight.

There are four vehicles for this transmission: look, touch, thought, and word. In the Tantric tradition, Shaktipat is thought to be the highest form of initiation, inviting immediate access to the divine energy within. It encourages the activation of what Tantra sees as three forms of kundalini: the prana-kundalini, which nurtures the physical body, the chitta-kundalini, which applies to our mind and emotions, and the para-kundalini, which pertains to our spiritual self. After the kundalini rises, this tradition suggests that it rests in a sacred space within.

Shaktipat is not without its work. Transmission by any method seldom occurs without first a purification process, teaching by a guru, and support afterward. The process does, however, both ignite and sustain the kundalini because of our increased awareness of the divine love already within our hearts. Seen in this light, the kundalini is an instrument of grace. The process of Shaktipat is similar to that of opening your heart-centered radiant kundalini. It seems all paths lead to our own divinity.

that emphasizes healthy living, the loving expression of emotions, the building of intimate relationships, and personal responsibility for one's actions and needs. The last thing I want to do is set someone up for a crisis or start a spiritual process that can't be integrated into everyday life.

I do not use this or any other form of kundalini activation on individuals struggling with serious mental or emotional health issues, however, as any strain might cause serious injury. I also don't initiate people who are merely seeking a kundalini thrill, perhaps desiring to only boost their sexual prowess or gain power over another. Tempting the Divine is not a good thing. Always, I remind myself that kundalini is a real power. It is a genuine spiritual energy. It won't harm us if we're genuine, but we must be genuine.

If you are seeking a kundalini transmission, I encourage you to seek out a guru or teacher who is willing to not only prepare you for the initiation but also see you through the process. Find someone you trust—someone who lives his or her espoused values and encourages you to live your own. Know that kundalini might skyrocket us to the heavens but is also meant to anchor us into our real lives. The more "real" the guru, the more authentic your own results will be.[58]

Be Your Own Guru: A Kundalini Self-Initiation

The safest way to work with your red kundalini is to start in your heart and activate your radiant kundalini first. Because the radiant kundalini always works for your highest good, you can safely activate it at any time. Awakening your radiant kundalini can serve as a method of purification and preparation for a red kundalini awakening. If your serpent is already awake and rising, radiant kundalini can dampen its potential enflaming effects and quicken the personal enlightenment available through the golden kundalini.

Before you activate any kundalini, whether radiant, golden, or red, it's important to step back and reflect on your intention and your current needs. While the radiant kundalini is safe to awaken at any time, it *is* kundalini. To decide to rouse our kundalini is to make a life commitment. It is to acknowledge our divinity and to pledge to express ourselves in everyday life as the divine self that we are. It's to promise to see others in the same light and to share our light with them. These are life-changing decisions, and—no pun intended—are not meant to be taken lightly.

As the kundalini courses through us, it makes way for more love and grace. We actually become the love and grace we long for. The resulting alterations in attitude, behavior, and lifestyle are best integrated gradually and gently. This is why it is a good thing to preface our kundalini activation with thoughtfulness and preparation.

The following series of exercises allows you to safely activate your serpent kundalini by first initiating a radiant kundalini awakening and then sparking the golden kundalini before finally gently nudging your red serpent to life. While the exercises can certainly be conducted at one sitting, it is preferable that you take a break between each of the three activations and gratefully incorporate the kundalini just stimulated. These breaks can be days or even months apart. Ease, self-love, and simplicity—those are your criteria for deciding when to take the next step.

EXERCISE

Part I: Lighting the Radiant Kundalini

Start by breathing deeply into your heart area, asking the Divine to bring you into the center of the heart chakra, where your spirit dwells alongside the Spirit of the Divine. Now sense the eternal presence of the Divine as you surrender to this oneness. You hear a voice that asks, "Are you willing to serve your higher purpose? To be loved? To share love?"

If you affirm with a yes, you begin to feel a slight pulsation, and through your mind's eye, perceive a bright white light that glimmers forth from the center of your heart. Soon the center of each of your chakras begins to glow as well, and you know yourself as completely loved and divinely supported. You now slip into the encompassing love of this divine energy—of this, your own divine light—and invite the Divine to assist you with bringing it through every aspect of your body and your life. Know that your intuition will tell you when to climb further along the stairway to heaven and proceed with the inflow of your golden kundalini.

Part II: Lighting the Golden Kundalini

Breathe deeply and enjoy the warm glow of your radiant kundalini, basking in this sensation before asking the Divine to active your golden kundalini. With a rush, you sense a golden, liquid light surrounded by a bright white river of light flood from above into your crown chakra. You feel like you are a lightning rod for personal enlightenment as this golden flow swirls down through your chakras, through your legs and feet, resting for a moment in your tenth chakra, under the ground. Here, it blends with the earth's various elements before it spreads out and, like a fountain moving upward, travels through the entirety of your auric field. Reaching your ninth chakra, about an arm's length above your head, this golden energy is cleansed by the sky and journeys downward again.

On its way, this time it is kissed by the radiant kundalini, which is now emanating from each of your chakras. Enraptured with the radiant kundalini, your golden kundalini swirls up, down, and around you, and you begin to become the spiritual self that it invites you to be. You can now choose to fully experience the resultant golden self until the time when your intuition encourages you to merge with the red kundalini that is your power and passion.

Part III: Lighting the Red Kundalini

Radiant and golden, you have been transforming into the being of light you have always been. It is now time to fully light the flame of your serpent, or red, kundalini, the empowering force that bolsters your purpose and passions.

Breathe deeply and feel the Divine's smile upon you. Your radiant self glimmers and glows. The golden energy of divinity pulses within. Acknowledge the downward flow of this golden light, which falls from the sky into your body.

This time, upon reaching your first chakra, the golden kundalini activates your serpent kundalini, and the bright red snake of desire, power, and femininity rises up, even as the golden kundalini continues to shimmer downward.

The red kundalini merges with the radiant and golden and transforms into a bronze color. It soothes, awakens, fuels, and nourishes, delivering every positive attribute of the other two kundalinis into every single chakra, as well as every cell and organ in your body. Once reaching the head, the serpent kundalini now shoots upward into the ninth chakra, falls down through your auric field, enters your tenth chakra, and continues upward.

You are a spiraling ball of swirling, nourishing, bright ribbons of light. Your spirit, happily held within the Holy Spirit, now manages reality for you. You breathe deeply, ready to deeply embody the physical, emotional, mental, and spiritual well-being delivered through these three kundalinis.

You may repeat this exercise anytime you feel you need to.

Everyday Enlightenment:
Principles for a Divine Daily Life

*We are responsible for what we are, and whatever
we wish ourselves to be, we have the power to make
ourselves. If what we are now has been the result
of our own past actions, it certainly follows that
whatever we wish to be in future can be produced by
our present actions, so we have to know how to act.*

—Swami Vivekananda

Once we've experienced a kundalini awakening, is
our life now transformed? Certainly. But even butterflies have to land on solid land, if only to sip nectar, rest a bit, and maybe chat with fellow butterflies.
In the same vein, there's a saying about what happens before enlightenment:

Chop wood, carry water.

There's another saying about what occurs *after*
enlightenment:

Chop wood, carry water.

It is common to believe that once we are enlightened, our life completely changes. Not so. It's also

tempting to believe that our job is done, but this is anything but the case. Integration is an ongoing process; as the Zen proverb wisely states, "After enlightenment, the laundry." It is more like one leg of a journey has ended and the next leg has begun. The total kundalini process is like going on a trip around the world. Imagine you start in Dubuque, Iowa. You purchase an open-ended airline ticket, one that lets you fly anywhere you want, whenever you want; you pack your suitcase and take off. The only thing you are absolutely sure of is that you are never going to return to Dubuque, Iowa. Imagine further that your goal is to learn about sculpture, a similar goal as that of freeing your true self from an imprisoning life.

On the first stage of your journey, you fly to Paris and are taught about the lifestyle necessary to become an artist: what to wear, how to eat, how to select the right tools and marble. This is comparable to purifying and preparing yourself for the kundalini process. You now integrate the knowledge into your life and journey on.

Next you fly to Italy, and you study with a teacher who shows you how she sculpts. You suddenly realize that you also can become a great artist. This is the equivalent to the kundalini awakening. This part of the teaching must also be integrated.

Then you fly off again, this time to Moscow, where you apprentice with an experienced sculptor. First, you chip away on a preliminary work, and over time, you finally create your masterpiece. You have "risen."

Are you done? No. You turn over your flight coupon and read the small print: FINAL DESTINATION, DUBUQUE, IOWA. You now fly back to your starting point and learn how to be a world-class sculptor in an everyday town.

Energetically, integration is part of every stage of enlightenment. During purification, we must adapt to the idea of change. We must become accustomed to thinking that we are responsible for these changes. During the preparation stage, we have to incorporate our new standards and attitudes and live by them. During the awakening, we must quicken our ability to shift, flow, and learn, instituting different ideas as we go. During the rising, we have to draw on our integration skills even more speedily, as each day might bring a new and different opportunity. One day we are cold and get out our long underwear and sweaters. The next day we are hot; now we get out our shorts and sandals. When finally we reach the plateau stage of the kundalini experience, we realize that we are the same person we have always been, just more so. Now we have to get used to that idea—and sustain everything we have learned and become. We must "walk our talk," as the Lakota would say. And we must feel our feelings.

Integrating Emotions: Finding Freedom in Feeling

One of the most common questions I hear about kundalini reactions is what to do with the emotions. The simplest (and perhaps most profound) answer I can give is this: *feel them.*

Having said that, the process gets a little more complex and can take a great deal of courage. Enlightenment is not for cowards.

I have been dismayed by how many individuals are told that they are not "doing spirituality right" because they have feelings. In fact, a woman client of mine who had experienced a kundalini awakening shared that she was embarrassed about how many more feelings she had had since becoming "enlightened." She had been told that a true sage is able to completely detach.

I have not found this approach among the great kundalini authorities, Eastern or Western. In my view, this attitude is an off-shoot of the patriarchal nature of many Western religions. Stripped of the divine feminine aspect, these religions have also been sanitized of emotion, true passion, and the importance of relationship and connection. Opening to kundalini provides equal access to the feminine and the masculine energies, the intuitive and the logical, the physical and the spiritual, and the emotional and the thoughtful. This is about relationship, about connection. Our ability to be intimate, internally, with others and with the Divine, is dependent on our ability to be emotionally vulnerable.

Relationships bring up emotions. A successful kundalini awakening and integration involves continual relationship interactions. This means we will probably experience even more involvement with our emotions as we proceed toward enlightenment.

An emotion is actually composed of two parts: a feeling and a thought. Together, a feeling and a thought create "energy in motion," or emotion—the energy we need to get and keep moving. Feelings speak for our body. They tell us what we need. If we listen to others' feelings, we are able to perceive what they need. As a language, each feeling carries its own message. Following are a few examples:

> **Anger:** I need boundaries.
>
> **Fear:** This situation is threatening, and I need to move toward or away.
>
> **Sadness:** I cannot sense love right now, and I would like to.
>
> **Happiness:** I can sense the love present, and I want to increase it.
>
> **Disgust:** This is not good for me, and I need to get rid of it.
>
> **Guilt:** I have goofed up and need to have more integrity.
>
> **Shame:** I think I am bad, and I need to let in more love.
>
> **Blame:** I think someone else is bad, and I need to forgive him or her and myself.

Thoughts form the basis of beliefs. Beliefs are great—as long as they don't get stuck inside of an emotion and continue to recycle to our detriment. The thought "bees make honey" and "honey makes me happy" will give us a joyful, tingly feeling when we see a bee. Thinking "bees sting" and "pain makes me sad" could cause us to run away whenever we see a bee.

Emotions arise because they help us make decisions. When the existing emotion is not helpful, we need to reframe it. How can we enjoy a garden if we run from every bee we see?

I can promise that a kundalini process will bring up emotions—probably more than you knew could exist. How beautiful! When we feel our feelings and listen for the true message, the Divine smiles. When we separate truth from fiction and operate from emotions that support rather than detract from our lives, the Divine beams.

I usually recommend that my clients practice these five steps when emotions arise—especially strong ones, which will present us our deepest learning.

1. Accept the emotion.
2. Feel it.
3. Listen to it: what is its gift?
4. Ask for divine input.
5. Be open to meeting the need under the emotion.

These five steps can help you heal and flourish through the emotional states the kundalini process elicits.

The Living Principles of Kundalini

The ancient yogis never meant for kundalini to be relegated to an ashram or lost to the everyday person. The idea of yoga, a practice wrapped around kundalini, is one of self-discovery, a continual exploration of life by the living of it.

According to yogic understanding, we already are the self we think we must become, whatever stage of the kundalini process we're enjoying. Whether we're concentrating on purifying, coping with a rising, inviting an awakening, working on integration, or doing a little of all four, we are already our real selves; we might, however, be unaware of this fact. Consequently, we are not experiencing optimum health, joy, and self-realization.

To help us manifest ourselves authentically, Patanjali's Yoga Sutras defined the Eightfold Path, principles for pursuing enlightenment while living life. Two of the eight paths, the *yamas* and the *niyamas*, are composed of ten ethical precepts that invite peace within ourselves, within our families, and within the community. When we find practical ways to employ these ten principles in our daily lives, we begin to embody the spirit of kundalini, as yoga expert and author Donna Farhi says in her book *Yoga Mind, Body & Spirit.*[59] These principles will help you create an appropriate and dynamic response to your kundalini, as well as an overall life plan that directs your inner energy toward outer goals—and invites outer life experiences that match your inner self.

Ten Principles for the Good Life

The yamas are concerned with ways to use our energy (including kundalini) in relationships. The niyamas increase our soulfulness and ability to make ethical choices. The combined ideas enhance our success at our endeavors.

What is success in terms of health, relationship, and work? It is not about having a perfect body. Nor is it about creating constantly calm relationships. (If it were, no one would have children.) Nor is it about having control of massive amounts of money, huge mansions, and an unlimited succession of servants. Life might hand us moments of any or all of these so-called measures of success, but what really matters is who we are and how we express this self on a daily, moment-to-moment basis. As you read through the ten principles, consider how they might provide insights for the real reason you are alive—the living of your divine life.

Yamas: Wise Characteristics

The yamas help us cultivate wisdom in all things we do. Here is a plain and simple presentation of each characteristic, along with a few tips on integrating them into your kundalini practice.

(1) Compassion for All Living Things (Sanskrit: *Ahimsa*)

An adherence to nonviolence, this concept is not about being a pacifist. Instead, it encourages us to abstain from criticism, judgment, and prejudice directed at both ourselves and others, as well as everything in the natural world. The attitude of harmlessness is not an excuse for repressing or denying the so-called negative emotions. Every unsettling sensation can be a call for love—to give, receive, or become the love that we are.

An easy way to further the practice of ahimsa is to catch yourself when thinking mean thoughts. When you can't, get thee to a mirror. Really. Stare into the eyes of the beautiful person looking back at you. Now speak those previously muttered judgments aloud. Watch your reaction. Notice the hurt and pain. Now say "I'm sorry" and start over. Speak from love instead of fear.

(2) Commitment to Truth (Sanskrit: *Satya*)

Central to satya is a single truth: honesty. This is the secret to healthy relationships of every sort, whether they be with a lover, child, parent, business associate, or even a pet. Anything less than being truthful harms the self and others.

How do we know "truth"? We start within our hearts, cultivating an awareness of our inner values. Internal integrity leads to external ethical behavior. Sometimes following our truth is hard. We might have to leave a bad relationship. We might have to risk being rejected by our "crowd" for refusing to gossip or drink. If we listen to our true self, however, we will know what to do—and what *not* to do.

One of the ways I commit to truth is by using the Freeze-Frame method to read what's really in my heart. Doc Childre of the Institute of HeartMath in Northern California developed this technique to reduce stress, but it also opens us to our inner knowledge. Consisting of five simple steps, synthesized here, it also helps us live from higher truths, including faith, hope, and love.

1. Disengage from stressful thoughts and feelings.

2. Focus on the heart area, bringing your breath in through your heart (fourth chakra) and sending it out through the solar plexus (third chakra).

3. Activate a positive feeling, such as appreciation for someone you care about.

4. Ask yourself what might be an effective attitude or action for balancing your system (and decide to take action later, if you need to).

5. Sense and sustain your change of perception or feeling.[60]

(3) Not Stealing (Sanskrit: *Asteya*)

All misuse and abuse arises out of a feeling of lack of abundance. We feel as if we do not have enough. We make happiness contingent on external circumstances and material goods. Following the advice of asteya begins with refusing to accept anything that is not freely given and to not give ourselves away needlessly.

If we "give ourselves away" as an adult, it is often because we unconsciously formed a codependent bargain with another person, usually Mom or Dad, when we were young.

A codependent bargain is an energy contract that psychically looks like a garden hose that energetically attaches us to another person. Energy flows two ways through this connection so that we can swap energy with someone else. These connections are usually established for survival purposes, such as: "I'll give you my life energy (kundalini) in exchange for you loving me/keeping me alive/feeding me/not rejecting me."

Frequently, the cost of the connection is our own life energy. Moreover, what we gain in return is usually another's negative energy—feelings, ideas, problems, or even diseases that interfere with our life. Not only does this connection continually renew itself, but it also becomes our model for relating to our subsequent life partners.

While we can establish these connections—or cords, as they are often called—between any of our chakras and another's, first-chakra bargains are the most detrimental. The first chakra is the in-body source of most of our kundalini, or raw life energy. When this life energy is siphoned away in a codependent bargain, we can become so disempowered and exhausted that we are often unable to actualize our life purpose. By giving away our life energy, we are actually stealing it from ourselves.

If you think you have a codependent bargain with someone else, consider working with a trained professional. You can also employ prayer or meditation to intuitively examine your chakras for cord-age. If you perceive one, ask the Divine to help you determine the origin of this bond, the nature of it, and the reason you might have unconsciously believed you needed it. Feel how you felt at the time of its inception and then ask for further insight about how to forgive yourself and all others involved. Now ask the Divine to provide you (and the other/s) with a true source of energy—divine love—as you release this attachment. Ask that both of you be united fully with the Divine and that your own life force be safely renewed and allowed to flow where it needs to, within and around your body.

(4) Merging with the One (Sanskrit: *Brahmacharya*)

This precept is usually considered a call to celibacy. Being celibate is not equivalent to sexual suppression; rather, it is about using our sexual energy for regeneration. Manipulating or using others with sex, or even sexual energy, creates pain, jealousy, and hatred. Our goal in raising our kundalini is to merge with the Divine. We can do so within the context of a loving earthly relationship or not. The ethical standards are the same.

For guidance, I like to turn to the truth of Tantric kundalini, which recognizes the feminine and masculine energy within each individual. Most Tantric texts outline eight aspects of intercourse, which guide a couple from developing sexual thoughts in the brain through full physical intercourse. These steps include activities such as thinking about sex, sharing words, playing games, touching each other, and more. Having sex is the last ingredient.[61] Think about eight steps that would enable you to have truly "safe sex"—sex that isn't hurtful, abusive, or a power play. The ultimate rule is this: if we follow our true value system in sex, we will naturally value our partner and want to be valued by our partner.

(5) Not Grasping (Sanskrit: *Aparigraha*)

Holding on and being free are contrary states of being. Our ego is trained to manipulate in order to hold on to something or gain security. Sometimes the more certain we try to make ourselves, the less adaptable we become and the less secure we really are. To resist change by grasping is to stop transforming. What matters is what is essential—appreciating what we have and who we are.

Want a demonstration of how this principle works? Think of a problem. Now hug your arms to your chest. Imagine yourself in the center of a circle of loving friends and angels. When you have your arms folded over your heart, it is difficult for them to help you, isn't it? It is also hard for your kundalini to keep rising.

Now extend your arms and throw your chest out. Look what happens! Your visible and invisible friends can hold your hands. It is also so much easier for your life force to rise and fill you with light and love. What might happen if you walked around with this much love in your heart, your hands open to what the world has to give?

Niyamas: Codes for Soulful Living

Following are descriptions of the niyamas, the yogic codes for the spiritual life, and how practicing them encourages a healthy, kundalini-filled life experience.

(6) Purity (Sanskrit: *Saucha*)

Pure living involves cleanliness. There are many ways to keep ourselves clean. These include taking care of our body, mind, and the environment. Healthy food and water are only two parts of the formula. We become not only what we eat, but also what we see, read, and who we associate with.

Adhering to this precept is one of the keys to inviting a healthy relationship with kundalini energy. Pure, organic, nonchemically influenced food and water nurtures our cells but also assists in toxin removal and prevents waste buildup. Physical blockages, like energetic blocks, can inhibit the upward spiral of the kundalini and create damaging side effects, such as illness, emotional reactivity, and loss of sexual control. More ideas on pure living are featured later in this chapter.

(7) Contentment (Sanskrit: *Santosha* or *Santosa*)

To be content is to be satisfied with where we are. Contentment is not the same as complacency or happiness. We should not tolerate abuse, nor should we believe we are always going to be joyful. By accepting the current situation, however, we sustain hopefulness by inviting it to become something greater.

Here's a really fun way to experience santosha. It starts with chocolate.

Most likely, you already like chocolate, but you may not know that it—like everything—can be energetically programmed for a higher effect. In fact, a new brand called Intentional Chocolate, infused with positive intentions, has been proven to enhance mood, general well-being, and focus, and to reduce fatigue and stress in a double-blind, placebo-controlled experiment.[62] Your natural love of chocolate can be transferred into situations that are less than appealing.

There are three stages to this experiment.

First, select a choice piece of chocolate. Holding it, think of the kundalini energy in your heart and pour all the goodness into the chocolate. Now eat the candy, taking time to savor it.

Next, try the same thing with a food that you do not like. "Yuck," you think, holding the food. Suspend judgment and focus on your heart before empowering the food with all the positive qualities you can embrace about your true nature. Concentrate on excellence while tasting the previously undesirable food. Does it taste different?

Finally, select a situation, person, or activity that you have never enjoyed. Deliberately participate in an interaction, but before fully engaging, follow the flow of your kundalini energy into your heart. Infuse the situation with all the love, goodness, and virtue that lie within your heart. Notice your feelings. Is there more contentment?

Continue this practice in all you do.

(8) Burning Enthusiasm (Sanskrit: *Tapas*)

Tapas means "fire." In yogic terms, this niyama calls us to direct our fire toward a good cause in a disciplined manner. Conviction and excitement generates movement.

It is not hard to produce energy for things or activities we like. It is more challenging to do so for things and activities we do not like. How about those house chores that you keep delaying? Or filing that large stack of papers in your home office? Discipline is sometimes the only way to turn up the flame, ignite a passion, and, in the end, get something done.

The key to tapas is really a form of disciplined awareness. *When we are in the moment, whichever moment it is, we bring all of ourselves to a task. When we apply all of our being to something, we become all that we can be in that moment.*

To transform a dreadful activity into a task of joy, select a job that you hate doing but that must be done. It might fall under the homemaking or landscaping category—like cleaning the bathroom or removing dog poop from the lawn. It could involve a personal habit, like scheduling dates or ironing your clothes for work. It could also mean buckling down on a work project in which you find little merit. Whatever task you select, take a few moments before starting and breathe your kundalini energy upward through your body, practicing safe and gentle techniques. Access the spiritual energy atop your head and merge the physical and spiritual energy in your heart. Then throw your whole heart into the chore.

(9) Self-Study (Sanskrit: *Swadhyaya*)

Our souls are naturally drawn to activities that reveal our true nature, whether those activities are hobbies, work, or simple expressions of life. We may not even know that by engaging in these activities we are engaged in self-study.

For a pursuit to be considered soul study, we must persist with it regardless of the outer or inner resistance or problems that arise. By doing so, we learn about our strengths and also our limitations. Often the pursuit reveals our fragmented self or soul, which we can then seek assistance to reintegrate into a divine whole.

As we form a relationship with kundalini energy, we also create a relationship with the various aspects of our self. These aspects can be represented by the chakras, each of which represents a certain quality of being. For instance, our first chakra corresponds to our physical self, and our second chakra relates to our emotional and creative self. As the kundalini courses through a particular chakra, it accentuates the related self and its various strengths, limitations, or needs. If we desire, we can now focus on that particular self and change what needs to change, heal what needs to heal, and embrace and accept what simply is.

Kundalini isn't trying to transform each of these individuated selves into a perfect human specimen; rather, it increases our self-awareness and invites us to make different choices, if desirable. This is an ongoing process, but we can practice the art of swadhyaya, or self-study, and gain optimum benefits through an exercise such as the following:

Select an activity and deliberately observe each of your "chakra selves" as you undertake this task. You can study each of these aspects, or selves, one at a time, while carrying out the project, or do the project several times and monitor a different chakra each time. For instance, I might choose to study my chakra selves while working in the house. How is my first chakra, my physical self, relating to the project? Does my verve pick up when I'm moving around furniture, only to dip down when I'm scrubbing the toilet? Does my second-chakra self perk up when I'm redecorating a room and get depressed when I'm vacuuming? As I move through my efforts, either in one fell swoop or during separate cleaning episodes, I watch for each chakric reaction.

I might figure out that I like being innovative and creative, but I hate dealing with dirt. I can now decide how to best deal with my tendencies. Maybe I can add more play to every task or put one chakra self in charge of the most dull endeavors. Maybe I can even hire someone to do the worst work. By being ruthlessly observant and honest, I better understand myself and can act accordingly.

I encourage you to choose an activity that will enable this type of soul study and watch each chakra self as it performs the related tasks. Any chakra system will work for this. I provide an outline for my own extended twelve-chakra system in chapter 2, in case you want to really explore all your character traits.

First Chakra	Physicality/Manifesting
Second Chakra	Emotionality/Creativity
Third Chakra	Mentality/Administrative
Fourth Chakra	Relating/Healing
Fifth Chakra	Verbalism/Communication
Sixth Chakra	Visioning/Strategy (and Foreseeing)
Seventh Chakra	Prophecy/Spirituality
Eighth Chakra	Shamanic/Mysticism

Ninth Chakra	Harmonizing/Idealism
Tenth Chakra	Naturalism/Connection to Ancestors and Nature
Eleventh Chakra	Command of Forces/Leadership
Twelfth Chakra	Mastery/Personal to Self

(10) Celebration of the Spiritual
(Sanskrit: *Ishvara Pranidhana*)

When we celebrate the spiritual self, we open a doorway for the sacred. Using ritual, celebration, solitude, or sacrament opens us to our true self. It also helps us examine our sorrows, regrets, or bitter moments for the sweetness that can lie beneath. The trick is to distinguish the difference between willingness and willfulness. Are you willing to open to the Divine's will, or are you simply willing the Divine to become "full of you"? It's easier to discern the difference if you "go to God" with your concerns.

Try setting aside a time, at least once a day, to ask the Divine for input about how to live a kundalini-infused life. You might also set aside a special space in which to connect; you might establish an altar space, choose a particular place to meditate, or sit under a special tree. You could read devotionals, stretch, write poetry, or draw funny pictures. You can use prayer, which involves sending a request to the Divine; meditation, which involves opening yourself to receiving answers from the Divine; and contemplation, which is simply basking in the presence of the Divine. This is your time to touch the omniscient and lean into the absolute.

God Glasses

All of the ten living principles interweave with this exercise. Spend a few moments every day wearing a special pair of "God glasses." These are eyeglasses made especially for you. When you wear them, they enable you to see the world—and yourself—through the eyes of the Divine. You can wear these glasses as often and for as long as you like.

These special eyeglasses will also help you compose a practical plan for a kundalini-embracing life, the core ingredients of which are covered in the next section.

Breaking Through the Koshas: Following the Ayurvedic Stages of Enlightment

As our kundalini evolves, nurtured and fed by the masculine and spiritual elements and a healthy approach to life, it enables us to break through five distinct barriers to enlightenment, called *koshas* in Ayurveda. Koshas are sheaths, or encasements, around our soul. Breaking through these different koshas is done in stages, progressing from practical to spiritual.

Here is a brief description of these five koshas and the applications of higher force, called *agni*, that enable this transformation. I draw from David Frawley's book *Yoga & Ayurveda* as well as my own studies and experience.

Personally, I believe that agni is an accessible form of the Divine and that kundalini in any form or by any name—including what I call the red, golden, and radiant kundalinis and others call the Holy Spirit, chi, or life force—are aspects of this source energy. The existence of agni suggests that kundalini is a divine light, one of the faces of the Divine expressing to and through it. As this higher force enters each kosha, it provides us the energy and impetus needed to purify and transform ourselves in specific ways. This metamorphosis isn't intended to change us, but rather to enable us to be our true selves.

Annamaya Kosha: Known as the food sheath, this is the stage when we concentrate on right eating and speaking, focusing on what we are taking in and also what we are putting out.

Pranamaya Kosha: The pranic sheath is the stage when we employ proper breathing to raise our consciousness and also focus on truthful speech.

Manomaya Kosha: In this stage, the outer mind sheath, we turn to matters of our inner mind to digest impressions and weave them into grander stuff with our imagination.

Vijnanamaya Kosha: During this stage, the sheath of intelligence, we access our powers of discernment to operate with integrity and morality.

Anandamaya Kosha: Here is the sheath of the fire of love. We now seek love rather than lust or desire, igniting the flame of our deepest wishes, highest motivations, and innermost aspirations. We emerge from this stage inflamed in the joy of embracing wisdom.

Beyond the fifth kosha, we apply ourselves to two more levels of development. The first is *chidagni*, the fire of consciousness, which depends on self-awareness. Essentially we must light our lives with the brilliant flame of the true self. The second stage is *brahman*, or the fire of being. This supreme reality acknowledges that the universal light and our personal light are the same. We can now light the way for others. We can now achieve the end result of a kundalini rising: loving service.

Ingredients for a
Kundalini-Infused Life

The best six doctors anywhere
And no one can deny it
Are sunshine, water, rest, and air
Exercise and diet.
These six will gladly you attend
If only you are willing
Your mind they'll ease
Your will they'll mend
And charge you not a shilling.

—Nursery rhyme quoted by Wayne Fields, *What the River Knows*

Kundalini energy can be directed toward any end, good or bad. When encouraged to flow toward our spiritual center, it will inevitably arrive there, bringing the rest of us with it. The more we train our kundalini toward higher ends, the easier it becomes to make decisions based on love, hope, and truth. Bad habits, cravings, and addictive tendencies begin to slide away.

Intention is the principle that directs our energy. *Intention follows attention.* If you obsess about what bothers you, including problems, issues, or angers, your perception will reinforce your challenges. They'll grow stronger. You'll become unhealthier. If you attend to positive goals, such as achieving optimum health, satisfying relationships, and meaningful work, you will achieve these. You'll become healthier. Your kundalini will reinforce your attitude either way.

The following section introduces activities that allow us to apply the ten living principles—the yamas and niyamas, covered in the last section—to our everyday lives. These activities are the cornerstone of every part of the kundalini process, from purification to integration. Practical and doable, they encourage the kundalini to support our best health and highest functioning.

Each recommendation is explained as a "proper" way to act. The word *proper* is not to be confused with perfection. Instead, it relates to the idea of suitability. Something that is suitable "suits us." It fits us hand in glove, protecting, decorating, and augmenting our lives. To enable enlightenment, our behaviors, actions, thoughts, attitudes, emotional expressions, relationships, and work must reflect our true self. The word *proper*, therefore, acknowledges that we have a right to act and live in such as way that respects and honors our inner self.

Proper Diet

The most important way to ensure a healthy kundalini experience is through diet. A suitable diet involves eating pure and nutritious foods, which are those that contain a high amount of prana, or life energy. A basic rule of thumb is that the closer a food is to its own life force origin, the better it is for you. For instance, just-harvested carrots will carry more prana than canned carrots.

When selecting protein and milk sources, consider the number of hormones, antibiotics, and other additives, as well as the state of the protein source when it was butchered, milked, or raised. Undue stress raises the levels of natural cortisone and adrenaline in animals, and these hormones become a part of your energy when you eat the animal products. No matter what your preferred food or beverages are, you are always better off with luminous foods— those that exclude additives and preservatives.

An effective way to assist our kundalini climb and healing prowess is to eat a chakra-based diet. As chapter 2 explained, the kundalini can get stuck in blocked chakras. We can entice it to rise in a smooth, healthy way by eating the foods related to various chakras. Deanna Minich, author of *Chakra Foods for Optimum Health*, suggests special foods to support the seven in-body chakras. Here are some of Minich's recommendations:

> First chakra: Eating issues often come from the desire
> to protect yourself. This chakra thrives when you eat

with others. Try foods for grounding and protection: protein, minerals, root vegetables, edible and medicinal mushrooms, and red-colored foods.

Second chakra: This chakra opens us to flow, or movement, including the flow of our emotions. We may become prone to overeating to stifle our emotions. Spend time creating your meal and paying attention to your senses when eating. Use foods for flow and feelings: fats and oils (especially those rich in omega-3s), fish, tropical fruits, seeds, nuts, and orange-colored foods.

Third chakra: This chakra transforms energy. That is why we need to keep its flame bright. It goes out when we deplete ourselves with sugars, soft drinks, and artificial sweeteners. To reignite your energetic fire, try low-glycemic carbohydrates, including complex carbohydrates, fiber, whole grains, legumes, and yellow-colored foods.

Fourth chakra: Sometimes we give more than we receive, and we eat to make up the balance. When we share food in a mutual exchange (and with love), we become healthier. This chakra flourishes when we express gratitude when eating, donate to food banks, and infuse love into our nourishment. Foods for love and compassion are vegetables, sprouts, raw foods, foods rich in chlorophyll, and green-colored foods.

Fifth chakra: This chakra is where our food first enters our body, as well as the energy center related to our breath and words. This chakra becomes imbalanced if we do not clearly articulate our food choices or if we are not mindful of how we take in our food. Eat mindfully, chew carefully, and get rid of distractions to create optimum fifth-chakra conditions. Focus. Foods for communication and truth are sea vegetables, soups, sauces, juices, and fruits.

Sixth chakra: This chakra loves it when we listen to our intuition rather than external pressures or our intellect. Foods for intuition and insight include herbal tea, blackberries, and blueberries.

Seventh chakra: This is our site of interconnection, deeper meanings, and the essential. Eating is a divine act. Eat foods that create a connection between the body, mind, and soul, as this act will underscore the purpose of the seventh chakra, the integration of all aspects of our self with divinity. Use foods that will foster unification and interconnection with the sun and moonlight, clean air, and unconditional love.[63] Do this by selecting foods that align with your value system. If you follow a spiritual path that is biblically based, consider diets described in the Old and New Testaments. If you support animal rights, consider becoming a vegetarian or vegan. Acknowledge divine grace before or after eating, using prayer or meditation. Bless your food and all who prepare it. Cook with a serene heart. As the Hindus shared thousands of years ago, the Divine is everywhere: food, sun, water, thoughts, care—and us.

Proper Exercise, Physical and Energetic

We need to m-o-v-e. Movement is the idea behind yoga asanas, but any exercise can help clear out blocks, encourage the upward climb of our life force, and integrate our spirit into our body. Waste matter and toxins build up over time, as do the negative energies from our self and others. These toxic blocks interfere with the flow of kundalini and create everything from physical traumas and illnesses to mental conditions. Moving every day alleviates energetic blockages and encourages the energizing effects of kundalini to circulate throughout the body and energy system.

Physical exercise is vital, but so is energetic exercise. As I've said, I believe that up to 80 percent of our irritating or even life-threatening conditions, from physical to mental, start with energies that we absorb from other sources. What others do not deal with becomes part of the energetic environment. If we are energetically codependent, we take on this free-floating flotsam. We might do this to help someone else, create safety for ourselves, or simply to alleviate the pressures of everyday life. These energies are not our own, and we are, therefore, unable to process them. What cannot be cleared becomes stuck. Exercise is one of the most vital methods for freeing ourselves from our own stress, as well as the stress resulting from this assumption of others' energies.

Proper Breathing

Every type of yoga teaches life-enhancing breathing techniques. That's why I keep stressing the importance of breathing, a topic covered throughout this book. Besides trying the breathing practices provided in chapter 6, remember to use abdominal breathing and abstain from chest breathing. Only the former enables diaphragmatic breathing, which allows the lungs to expand and contract. Also remember, the stronger the exhale, the more toxins are released.

Proper Habits

We have all developed patterns that leave us exasperated. The worse we feel about our bad habits, the harder it is to change them—even though we know that they interfere with our relationships, self-esteem, bodily functions, and spiritual well-being.

If we are really stuck, especially in an addiction, it is imperative to get help. Many therapists understand not only family dynamics but also the effects of soul issues and energetic problems.

I've found it helpful to pinpoint my own or my client's addictive tendencies to the causal chakra. This way, I can focus my kundalini on that particular chakra or determine exactly what outside help I need. Want to know which addictive tendencies are located in each chakra? On the following pages is a chart featuring the twelve-chakra system.

Chakra	Symptoms or Negative Habits
First	Addiction to hard drugs, alcohol, work, sex, exercise, cutting, sadistic or masochistic behaviors, spending, milk, fat, or meat. Chronic or frequent illness, frequent accidents. Debt.
Second	Addiction to gluten-rich foods, wheat, starchy carbohydrates, grain-based alcohol, chocolate, and certain or all emotions (as in emotionalism).
Third	Addiction to work, perfection, marijuana, caffeine, carbonated beverages, beer, corn-based alcohol, and corn-processed sugar.
Fourth	Addiction to Ecstasy (the drug), love (having to be in love all the time), specific relationships (persons you can't let go of), smoking, wine, sugar and sweets, and false sugars such as saccharin or aspartame.
Fifth	Compulsive talking or reading, compulsive overeating, and smoking or chewing tobacco.
Sixth	Self-hatred (as in poor body image) and compulsive worry about appearances. Addiction to chocolate and all mood-altering substances. Compulsive behaviors such as handwashing and criticalness.
Seventh	Addiction to "uppers" or "downers," and/or alcohol. Adherence to fanatic religion; use of prayer or meditation in order to avoid reality. Depression or anxiety.

Chakra	Symptoms or Negative Habits
Eighth	Addiction to substances that can be used in healing, such as tobacco, nicotine, and coffee. The shamanic personality absorbs others' issues and often uses addictive substances to buffer the side effects of these toxic physical and psychic energies.
Ninth	Poverty, scarcity, doing good for others to the point of hurting the self. The ninth-chakra personality is an idealist and can sometimes self-sacrifice too much.
Tenth	Using psychogenic mushrooms (as a drug). Outdoor exercise (such as hiking) used for escapism. Using a focus on animals or nature to avoid people. Addiction to root vegetables, nuts, or chemicals, including food additives, glues, or other human-made inorganics.
Eleventh	Negativity, power issues (as in having to be in control).
Twelfth	Immature behaviors and abusive relationships of any sort. Lack of meaning.

Proper Environment

Geopollution is a relatively new term that underscores the challenges of living—or trying to stay alive—in the current world. Several studies are proving that being continually bombarded by electromagnetic pollution—from power lines, computers, x-rays and microwaves, cell phones, and even plugged-in kitchen appliances—negatively affects us.

Some of us are more sensitive to these energies than other people are. If you are one of these ultrasensitive people, do some research and find out what you can do to alleviate some of your stressors. Sometimes it is as easy as unplugging electric appliances when you are not using them. Other times, you might need to consider relocation.

Another way to lessen environmental stressors is to transform your home into a sacred space. Noise can also be a huge environmental stressor. Too much noise can cause heart problems, ringing in the ears, high blood pressure, sleep disturbances, emotional imbalances, and immunological and metabolic disorders, according to a report by the World Health Organization.[64] The benefits of consciously activating our kundalini energy will not last long when we are exposed to blaring radios, screaming and yelling, loud televisions, or rock and roll pumped directly into our heads through our iPods' earbuds.

As part of a good environmental strategy, consider employing practices such as feng shui or *Baubiologie* (building biology), which show how to place objects to decrease negative and increase positive energies. Do not forget to spend some time outside every day.

Proper Expression

Emotional hygiene is important. Whatever feelings we incubate or explosively express will inevitably turn into a problem for others and ourselves. This applies to both feelings and thoughts; the latter is the subject of the next section.

On the one hand, we do not want to repress our emotions; otherwise, we'll become sick. Fortunately (kind of), a rising kundalini energy can trigger all unhealed emotional and physical traumas. Not only should we deal with these, but we should also want to. We deserve to be freed from the events or emotions imprisoning our soul. On the other hand, flinging our powerful emotions at others only injures our loved ones and us. The key is to experience, rather than only express, our emotions. Fully experiencing our emotions will open the flow of our kundalini and cleanse us of the beliefs that caused us to repress them in the first place. For tips on embracing and learning from our feelings, see the section "Integrating Emotions: Finding Freedom in Feeling" earlier in this chapter.

Proper "Impression"

Most of our supportive or destructive tendencies start as negative thoughts or beliefs that have been impressed upon us. In other words, we have all been repressed, depressed, compressed, and recessed by beliefs that do not serve us. Where do these unhelpful beliefs come from? Parents, ancestors, extended family, culture, friends, religion—you name it.

We are painfully unaware of most of the impressions that determine our reactions. Of the roughly 50,000 thoughts that we think each day, about 98 percent are exactly the same as those we had the day before.[65] Of these, about 80 percent are negative.[66] How can we clean up our unconscious thinking? In everyday life, we must manage the external information we expose ourselves to. We have choices. Abstaining from porn, the news, dark movies or books, and even negative conversation leaves us less to clean out later.

How about clearing out what's already inside? To accomplish an inner housecleaning, try the following advice from the Mayo Clinic:

(1) Identify your negative thinking. Common types include:
  - Filtering, or automatically screening, out positive aspects of a situation and concentrating instead on the negative twists
  - Personalizing, or blaming yourself even when you are not responsible
  - Catastrophizing, anticipating the worst
  - Polarizing, seeing only good or bad—no shades of gray

(2) Focus on positive thinking. Here are some new ways to think:
  - Check yourself. Evaluate your thoughts every so often and transform them from "not nice" to "kind."
  - Try humor. Smile and laugh. It helps.

- Adopt a healthy lifestyle. Exercise at least three times a week and eat a healthy diet.
- Connect with happy people. We become who we hang around. Negative people think they have no power to change their lives; do you want to think like that?
- Talk nicely to yourself. Do not say anything to yourself you wouldn't say to someone else, and remember to be kind to others![67]

Proper Stress Relief

Stress is more about our reaction to events than the events themselves. The entirety of the kundalini process invites stress relief in that it encourages us to stop, think, and reframe according to higher principles, such as the ten living principles shared earlier in this chapter.

Proper Relationships

We become like those with whom we associate. We also tend to treat others as what we think they are rather than who they actually are.

If we were hurt as a child or in an important relationship, we may think that everyone else is as hurtful as the perpetrator of the abuse. We might see every potential friend as the same person who gossiped about us in seventh grade, every possible girl- or boyfriend as an extension of an abusive parent. It is imperative that we conduct the personal-growth work necessary to clear up our past and see clearly in the present.

We do not return to the past to become trapped; we visit the past to free ourselves from the misperceptions that created alienation and unworthiness.

This cleansing is a process, one often necessary during both the kundalini purification and awakening stages. Quite simply, the more aware we become through the kundalini process, the more aware we are of our problems and projections. Achieving ease often requires a great deal of work.

We must consciously decide whom to hang out with on a daily basis. If we are trying to stop drinking, we have no business sitting around in bars or spending late-night hours with drinking buddies. If we want to be treated well, we have to treat ourselves with respect and commune with people who treat themselves respectfully.

As well, it's helpful to engage in the type of healing activities covered in chapter 3—activities for dealing with a spontaneous or challenging awakening. Performing regressions and doing our soul work and the like frees us from the past and opens us to the life and relationships we're dreaming of.

Proper Livelihood

There is the thought that a truly awakened person divorces him- or herself from the world and lives either in solitude or in selfless devotion to duty. For most of us, a kundalini awakening stimulates the opposite. We must be in the world, walking our talk.

Some people yearn for a true kundalini awakening because they want the icing on the cake, the gifts accompanying the experience. Upon reaching the crown chakra, the kundalini energy activates the siddhi, or magical spiritual gifts. Nearly every culture and religion promises the stirring of miraculous abilities upon union with the Divine. Jesus Christ performed healings, walked on water, and raised the dead; Buddha carried out the equivalent. While there are great powers—about forty siddhi, according to many Hindu sources—they are not the goal of enlightenment. Says Swami Sivananda, the siddhis are actually "obstacles to Realisation…He who runs after siddhis will become…a worldly minded man."[68] Naturally, we want to use our spiritual gifts in order to live meaningful work lives. But the gifts do not make us who we are; we make the gifts into what they can be. Ultimately, we are to serve through them.

Every one of the ten living principles is relevant to right livelihood. It does not really matter what we do for a living; what matters is how devoted we are to it. It does not matter how much money we make; what matters is that we accept payment and share with others. To receive fruits for our labors is to respect ourselves; to give to others is to respect them. It does not even make a difference if we have a job that reflects our "whole" self; what matters is that once we show up "on the job," we work with integrity.

The same is true of every part of our life. No matter who we are, we must show up to live it.

For Women Only
(And Our Feminine Selves)

History is herstory too.

—Unknown

We all know that men and women are different. One of my favorite series of books, which started with *Men Are from Mars, Women Are from Venus* by John Gray, describes the division between the genders by suggesting we might as well be from different planets. Men are from Mars, the planet of caves and fix-it gadgets. Women are from Venus, the planet of emotional squishiness. Where men think in lines, women reflect in circles. When men listen for facts, women talk for connection. Although we all have both masculine and feminine qualities, these gender differences are real, and they affect the relationship we have with kundalini. It's also vital to understand the energetic differences between the feminine and the masculine sides of reality, if only so we can fully benefit from the effects of kundalini.

In both genders, kundalini stirs up deep issues relating to love, power, respect, and sex, but it operates differently in a woman than it does a man, for two main reasons: first, a woman tends to run energy through different chakras than does a man. Second, a woman's bioenergetic development differs from a man's. Embrace these distinctions and the feminine within can contribute fully to the person that you are.

Women's Energetics: The Uniqueness of "Woman"

In my own work as a healer, I have discovered that kundalini stimulates different responses in women than men. One of the reasons is that women locate their consciousness in the "feminine" versus "masculine" chakras, thus stirring up a different set of issues and responses to kundalini.

Many healers believe that the even-numbered chakras are feminine in that they are receptive; they draw energy in. The odd-numbered chakras are masculine, sending energy out. The feminine chakras could be termed more magnetic than electric, more internal than external. (Some healers, including Rosalyn Bruyere, believe there are male and female chakras and that certain chakras are a mix of both, or transcendental.[69])

Because of energetic, societal, and religious programming, women operate more frequently from these feminine chakras. These chakras are internal, reflective, and intuitive in quality, rather than dominating, animated, and vigorous. Therefore, for women, rising kundalini will stir up more issues within the feminine chakras and, in particular, at least during its incipient rise, in a woman's second chakra. (In my twelve-chakra system, there are additional chakras beyond the seven in-body ones. The higher-numbered feminine chakras are eight [mysticism], ten [environmental], and twelve [personal mastery].)

The base of the sushumna is a meeting ground for the ida and the pingala nadis, which are respectively feminine and masculine. After stirring, however, a woman's kundalini immediately leaps into the second chakra, the focus of her body-based existence. It is here that she plays out an inner drama that determines the ultimate effectiveness of the kundalini. It is here she figures out what it means to be a woman responding to feminine serpent energy.

For Women:
Second-Chakra Specials

The second chakra is a haven of emotion and creativity, the chakra of connection and physical sensuality. When employed sexually, it engenders eroticism, the enjoyment and appreciation of the senses. Touch, taste, sight, tones, feeling, and sensations—these come together to ensure a connection with one's deeper self, as well as a bond with another.

The core of a woman's second chakra is her womb, the space of dreams and dreaming. Within the womb lies a gateway to the universe; it is an entry point for others' needs, feelings, and truths. The essential symbol of this chakra is water, which reflects women's ability to assume others' energies but also follow the flow of intuition to share love, compassion, and understanding. Years ago, Carl Jung, the famous therapist, noted this link between water, the second chakra, and women, declaring that the "second center...is intensely female, for the water is the womb of rebirth, the baptismal fount." He considered the moon to be a female symbol, the receptacle of the souls of the dead. Having received these souls, the moon, in turn, births the souls to the sun. Jung, therefore, attributed to women the power of rebirth, of creativity, of deep magic and mystery.[70]

Through the womb and the menses associated with it, women come to embrace the cycles of life itself—those cycles reflected in the living of a normal day and those described by the acts of birth and the guarantee of death. As shared by famous psychic Edgar Cayce, the second chakra is much more than it seems. He called it the "lyden," or seat of the soul, envisioning it as an encasement for the soul and, therefore, the soul's command center. According to Cayce, when the kundalini rises, it carries the soul with it, activating each higher chakra with the soul itself.[71] Thus, we could see women—Woman—as the spiritual divine, the one who carries the potential to bring new souls on earth and also initiate the soul into the body.

Most women have a difficult time thinking of themselves as divine. Most have been raised in cultures and religions that do not recognize the feminine as an equal or as a coequal aspect of the Absolute. In the Indus Valley, however, the feminine was always considered divine. The following of the Shakti gave her, the feminine, supreme authority of all creation, exceeding the power even of Shiva, Vishnu, Brahma, and other male gods. Her attractive form is linked with the inner workings of the universe.

By acknowledging the presence of a feminine divine and natural power within her body, a woman can tap into the creative and healing forces of the universe, not only for herself but also for loved ones, as well as the greater world. The power of the feminine self lies in the awakened second chakra.

What happens if there are too many encapsulated issues within a woman's second chakra—if she is unable to filter societal beliefs from spiritual truths? The most common symptoms include hormonal imbalances, fears about pregnancy, denying a personal desire for children (or, conversely, having more children than one can care for) in order to secure a life partner, loose or rigid sexual boundaries, the inability to let go and enjoy one's own body during sex or any other activity, overemotionalism, underemotionalism, absorbing of others' emotions, codependency, depression, anxiety, premenstrual syndrome (PMS), gluten or carbohydrate cravings or sensitivities, and intestinal disorders. While the kundalini might activate or amplify the issues, promoting these problems, it also encourages the release of powers that can heal them.

The effect of the kundalini is partially based on the development stage of the woman. I can't count how many times women have shared embarrassment at being different than the men around them. "I'm not as successful," "I'm getting too old to try for my dreams," "I have too many feelings," "I'd rather take care of my kids than climb the corporate ladder," or conversely, "In trying to keep up, I'm becoming a man." It's imperative to understand that a woman's bioenergetic development cycle is different than a man's. An awakening kundalini won't turn a woman into a man, but it will catch a woman up to her present "age" and help her become the whole person she is meant to be.

Women's Bioenergetic Development Cycle

What is this bioenergetic development cycle I speak of? It's one I have observed in the over thirty thousand clients I've worked with over twenty-five years. Loosely based on my twelve-chakra system, it reflects the different priorities of women at different ages. These main concerns are partially indoctrinated by society, largely due to biology, and are also reflective of a woman's role as the nurturer and creator in the world. These are the stages I have perceived:

Childhood: At this age, girls have partial freedom to
explore both feminine and masculine traits; this freedom
diminishes over time. Girls learn that safety involves being
nice so as to attract a man at a later date. They also learn
how to take on others' feelings to achieve this goal. They
develop a sense that it's more important to have personal
power than the power of a position, and personal power
is often reached by being loving and connected. Girls
become skilled at listening and responding to others' needs
and at appearing attractive.

Adolescence: Young women become aware that women's role in society entails having children; creating a home; providing for dependents; taking care of others' feelings, relational needs, and vulnerabilities; and appearing nice, kind, loving, and caring.

Age 21–35: At this age, women's goals include meeting men's fantasies, establishing a work life, finding the man, starting a family, and nesting.

Age 35–56: Women begin to question their soul calling, global issues, and leadership abilities. They now start to care for those outside of the family unit or friendship circle while still taking care of those within the nest. They may experience a crisis that stimulates a need for self-awareness, self-growth, and self-care. Questions arise about how to use personal power to help the self and not only others. They have become more concerned with being kind, which involves an authentic communication of truth, and less focused on being "nice," which is based on people-pleasing.

Age 56 and beyond: There is a call to personal mastery accompanied by an increased desire to access personal power and a loving nature and to open unawakened gifts, from creative to administrative to anything in between. This age opens the most internal and, if done correctly, external doors for success, material and otherwise, as the biological programming to take care of others recedes and the energetic systems are now, hopefully, completely open and interconnected.

Kundalini and Women's Bioenergetic Development Cycle

The kundalini, when activated, will meet a woman where she is, heal beliefs that don't match her true self, and bring her up to date, triggering the issues connected with her age in the bioenergetic cycle. A fifty-year-old female who is starting menopause when struck by the kundalini might start questioning her soul calling. She might suddenly become "less nice" as long-held resentments rise to the surface and she starts thinking about herself, not only others. She might be less prone to taking care of others' feelings, which can lead to friction with others. Her body, perhaps sadly neglected, will start demanding attention. In her case, what seems to be only menopause is so much more than hormones.

For instance, I worked with a fifty-five-year-old woman, a schoolteacher with an abusive husband, who had been undergoing a kundalini process for over five years. Her kundalini awakened the day her youngest son went to college. She reported that she felt an intense boiling energy start to rise through her pubic area and go straight to her heart, and she began shaking. While the physical symptoms abated after a few weeks, she informed me that she was never the same again.

She began saying no to her husband's demands to make every meal and keep the house perfectly clean while he sat on the couch. She joined a health club and lost thirty pounds. She visited her children at college by herself; previously she'd never traveled anywhere alone. She also started taking writing classes, in hopes of eventually becoming an author. This client simply needed support from me to continue to self-define. Her growth and progress had been stunted by dysfunctional belief systems and a lack of love from her partner.

I have found that kundalini often lends a helping hand to a woman or girl's maturation process, helping her "catch up," no matter her biological age. I once worked with a twenty-year-old woman raised by two alcoholic parents. Actually, the term *parent* was a misnomer; if anyone was the parent, it was my client, who had to cook, clean, and even start making money at age ten to order to take care of herself and the family. This young woman came to see me because she was experiencing subtle waves of heat in her body, as well as inspirational dreams. In them, various angels would appear and show her parts of her past, explaining the limitations of her parents and encouraging her to embrace her own truth and beauty. As well, the angels recommended that she leave home and forge a life of her own.

As we worked together, I aided this young woman's understanding of the reasons she was scared to step out alone. *It's hard to become an adult when you've never been a child.* Our work included her attendance at twelve-step programs and yoga classes, the latter because I suspected a kundalini experience. Eventually she applied for a scholarship at a local community college and, with the help of the administration, began a new career as a student—and as herself. Kundalini's presence was a necessary force for awakening this woman to the goodness of her feminine power.

Kundalini can strike a woman or a girl at any point in her life, even in the womb or early childhood. Sometimes, an infant is born with the feminine power already percolating. One of my clients, a young mother, brought her toddler daughter to see me. The child had been born with a thin, red line etched along her spine. It didn't seem to cause discomfort, and so the parents and physicians ignored it. But the little girl also had an amazing, if elusive, gift: if anyone was sad, ill, or down, she would put her hand on their forehead, and immediately the person would feel relief.

"Is my child normal?" asked the mother. "Is this God or the devil? Is this kundalini?" She added this last question because she had been exposed to Eastern religions. I could say that yes, this child is normal, if normal means gifted, special, and unique. Is this child's ability and the presence of the red line on her back an indication of fully activated kundalini? Maybe. No matter the label, she is a child of God, I explained to the mother—as we all are. I encouraged her to accept the child's gift but to raise her daughter as she might any child: with love, care, discipline, and integrity.

No matter what age we are when undergoing a kundalini uprising, we have nothing to gain but ourselves. Roles must be examined; if they do not fit, they might be lovingly updated or, sometimes, cast off. Self-images that contain or imprison us must be gently pried off so that we can see ourselves the way the Divine sees us. Behaviors that injure ourselves or others must be acknowledged and used as windows to our soul—a soul that longs to express itself and bring value to the world.

I have found that the most challenging (and even frequent) times for a kundalini awakening for females is when her hormones undergo predictable and typical shifts. This includes puberty, when a woman stirs inside the child; pregnancy and post-pregnancy, when a child emerges from a woman; and menopause, when a woman transforms into a wisdom keeper. These time periods share several factors, including the birthing of a new self and the release of an old way of being.

Gain and loss, nativity and death—the circle of life and light is mirrored in the arrival of the kundalini in the seventh chakra. Here, before the transformed kundalini takes residence in the sixth chakra, the maiden meets her man, and the two become one. This merging isn't without its pain or its loss. Aspects of the feminine are tempered or given up to make way for a different way of loving. Women cycle these acts of birth, death, and rebirth inside of themselves.

One of the ways I've assisted women through these challenges is to encourage the completion of the kundalini rise, no matter what age the woman is. Girls must be supported in retaining (or regaining) the innocence of childhood. If they are on the cusp of adulthood, I help them look for mentors or role models that represent the grace of womanhood. Young women need the same examples, with the additional empowerment that comes from seeing and owning their dreams. Midlife women might need to recycle their childhood and earlier adult years but require support in sharing their gifts in the world. Post-menopausal women are the wisdom bearers and often ready to begin second, third, or fourth careers—forms of work that care for the greater world, not only the home front.

In the process, I make sure that the feminine serpent completely shifts from the sixth to the seventh chakra before finally coming to rest in the sixth chakra. Many women unconsciously block this progression. They might feel edgy with masculine energy in general and so avoid letting the kundalini into the masculine chakras. Some avoid using or connecting with the masculine chakras in any way, in addition to preventing the kundalini from touching those chakras. The spiritually oriented, purpose-driven seventh chakra might be the most frightening to embrace because of the violent nature of God, who is usually depicted as male in most religions. Maybe women have bought into the societal prejudice that declares only men can succeed at life or in spirituality. Maybe leaving the feminine regime is unsettling; after all, the sixth chakra is the last feminine frontier in the body's chakra system. And perhaps they lack role models. Women have not been promoted to positions of spiritual or worldly authority for thousands of years; they have, therefore, not enjoyed the fruits of a spiritual awakening.

Whatever the case, I have found that many hormonal, emotional, and psychological challenges are soothed and even completely healed once a woman's kundalini transfers from the sixth to the seventh chakra. Because of this, I recommend that all women eventually make their way up the "rainbow path" to their pineal gland. If we become who we really are before maturity, we will enjoy every single state of our lives.

The Rainbow Path to Your Pineal Gland

In my experience, women in particular respond to color as a way to encourage the kundalini upward. The reason for this lies in women's affiliation with the second chakra, the home of color and texture. Following the rainbow path—the colors associated with each chakra—from the first chakra to the seventh chakra, home of the pineal gland, guarantees a woman full ownership of both her feminine and her masculine qualities.

The simplest way to guide the kundalini into each chakra is to start at the bottom and use color imagery to coax it upward, stopping always when there is resistance. Never pursue the next stage before you feel complete with the one you are in. Colors can be used during the kundalini process for healing, chakra clearing, and mood enhancement. Many of the tools for integrating kundalini into everyday life, such as guided visualization and environmental decorating, can make use of chakra-related colors or chakra-based foods. Wearing clothing or gemstones of a particular chakra color also allows you to tap into the power of that chakra.

First chakra: The gateway to life and death, the first chakra is where we decide what to keep and what to release. Red, the color of the first chakra, activates courage and physical energy.

Second chakra: Orange purifies and clears, assisting recovery from past abuse and assuaging emotions. It boosts the feminine libido and promotes the acceptance of a creative, powerful, sensual self.

Third chakra: Yellow activates male power and reduces imbalances resulting from inappropriate or abusive uses of power. It also stimulates the intellect.

Fourth chakra: Green encourages harmony, balance, freedom, and love for the self and others.

Fifth chakra: Blue enhances psychic and physical communications and encourages the understanding of higher spiritual principles.

Sixth chakra: Purple ushers in spiritual peace, balances hormones, and treats many compulsive behaviors. It also activates visual psychic perception.

Seventh chakra: White encourages spiritual development and an attitude of reverence and tolerance.

For Men Only
(And Our Masculine Selves)

He is a wise man who does not grieve for the things
which he has not, but rejoices for those which he has.

—Epictetus

We all have a feminine and masculine side, but men are presented with a unique challenge when it comes to kundalini. Men are in the odd position of becoming enlightened through a feminine energy, one housed in a very male chakra.

As we explore the male psyche, we'll discover that men run energy through what are often called the male chakras. Moreover, a man's bioenergetic development differs from that of a woman. To know what's exceptional about your gender from an energetic point of view is to invite the best from a kundalini process. It's also to rejoice in calling forth the best of the self.

chapter ten

Men's Energetics:
The Singularity of Man

As noted in the previous chapter, kundalini creates different effects in the two genders. Men, rather than women, enjoy their own particular reactions because they tend to live in the masculine versus feminine chakras.

The masculine chakras are the odd-numbered chakras, which are more outward oriented rather than inward oriented. Electrical (rather than magnetic) in nature, they are active, dominating, and driven. They spur men on to great deeds, lofty thoughts, and sometimes, physical activities that don't always serve them or others. When the kundalini awakens, its electrical energy supercharges the masculine chakras, which are already extraordinarily electrified. Potentially, this double intensity means that kundalini initiations can be more explosive for men than women. (In the twelve-chakra system, the higher masculine chakras are the ninth [global] and the eleventh [commanding].)

Wonder why the ancients continually warn against a "too sexual" or wild kundalini uprising? Well, most of these red flags were established by men, for men. When a woman's kundalini wakes up, it peers around her first chakra, yawns a time or two, and dances up to play in her second chakra. But when a man's kundalini awakens, it begins lunging around right in the first chakra, a highly physical, interactive land of red. Think about the color red and the images it induces: passion, physicality, anger, action, sex, doing, pushing. That's right—a kundalini rising is pretty much a nosedive into a swimming pool of evocative sensation.

The male chakras are all action based. The first chakra dominates primal needs and goals; the third, work success and power. The fifth chakra communicates and expresses, and the seventh, the goal of a kundalini rising, actualizes our spiritual purpose. A kundalini rising starts, however, in the first chakra, where the ida and pingala, female and male nadis, meet in the coccyx, the center of the first chakra, which is masculine.

For Men:
First-Chakra Fuel

The first chakra is a man's first home. Located in the hips and linked to the adrenals, it anchors his life energy and accentuates the need for safety and security. Every basic life requirement, including money, housing, sex, a primary relationship, and all other fundamentals of physical existence, starts with first-chakra energy. The self of a happy, thriving, prosperous man is securely attached to and rooted within a healthy first chakra.

Then comes the kundalini, a fire energy, beginning to burn inside a fire-based chakra. Buried issues transform into kindling, vulcanizing as the kundalini increases. You can't dig deeper than first-chakra issues or touch on more painful problems. What can erupt are the hardest issues to deal with: hurt, shame, abuse, ridicule, loss, lack of identity, relationship ruptures, abandonment, terror. If there's any reason to believe himself unworthy, a man will discover it within his first chakra.

If the subterranean issues are really hot, addictions develop or increase; addictions are simply a way to block out or avoid deeper pain. I've perceived that the first-chakra-related addictions lie on one of two sides of a fence. On the one side are the active addictions; these involve acting out with gambling, work, drugs, or sex. If the kundalini stimulates an even higher misuse of sexual behavior, such as promiscuity or the use of porn, there are obviously deeper issues that lie underneath. In these cases, sex, which should afford intimacy and connection, has been transformed into a method for feeling better, "blowing off steam," or gaining a false sense of power. The other side of the fence is an addition that is often not diagnosed: it's perfectionism. The "too good" man indulges in the fantasy of make-believe correctness. In this camp are men often considered the pillars of the community, the leaders in their worship halls, the ever-loving husbands or fathers. Some men attempt to live in both worlds, the acting out and the imploding in, and do great damage to themselves and their loved ones.

The goal of kundalini—the feminine goddess—is truth. It doesn't cause extremes, it announces them. As a man pursues his wounds and, simultaneously, his true self, he begins to feel. He begins to heal. He becomes caring, able to better measure actions against his inner values. He then understands that, underneath it all, he is what he wants to become. The role of the kundalini is to provide the unconditional love, the maternal strength, needed to live through the burn and begin the climb along the evolutionary ladder of the chakra system.

Men's Bioenergetic Development Cycle

A man's bioenergetic development, like a woman's, can be sequenced according to his age. This bioenergetic staging, established by societal norms, biological programming, and energetics, explains a man's priorities at different times. The kundalini's goal is to catch a man up with his specific age and encourage his full potential.

> Childhood: At this age, boys have partial freedom to explore both feminine and masculine traits; this freedom diminishes over time as boys learn how they fit in with these orientations. They learn that masculine identity is based on achieving financial security and a powerful position in society, and that being vulnerable comes at a high cost. In the end, it is important to be admired.

> Adolescence: The male role assumes the need to make money, provide for dependents, safeguard the home and nation, and appear strong, brave, and invulnerable.

Age 21–35: At this age, men are playing out of fantasies, driving hard to achieve career success, building their reputation, starting a family, "getting ahead," and beginning a last push to gain and solidify power.

Age 35–56: Men now question their soul calling, global issues, and leadership abilities. It's time to for them to complete the drive to power and monetary success before shifting to uncovering a deeper purpose. They are also stimulated by the desire to find true love, if they have not already. Depending on their internal integrity, they can feel compelled to become personally accountable and responsible for their actions.

Age 56 and beyond: Full maturation calls for making a real difference, which might require men to separate from their family or everyday concerns to serve in a higher capacity. They might experience a shift from egotism to altruism. This age can activate a man's ability to truly embrace and comprehend love for others, not only of the self.

Kundalini and Men's Bioenergetic Development Cycle

How might the kundalini affect, say, a fifty-year-old man? Yesterday he liked his job; today he doesn't. It lacks meaning. It seems stupid. Shame arises—shame at having "sold out"—and he starts to dream backward in time, to when he had real dreams, dreams about making a real difference. If he is in a relationship, he might start to wonder, "Do I love this person? Did I ever? If not, should I look for someone truly compatible, someone who can help me with my quest for higher service?" Questions such as these spur him into searching his past and immediate surroundings for responses that might have once fit, but are most likely somewhat mismatched at this point. Like the tuxedo worn at a teenage prom or the suit donned for a first job interview, what once seemed appropriate is tried on, and the man notices what's too tight or too loose. Roles, ideas, and even values pile up like discarded pieces of a wardrobe in this effort to figure out what he might still become.

The kundalini, in its feminine wisdom, keeps him seeking until he's decided that he's worth more than outdated values adopted from childhood or systems that have surrounded but never embraced him. Some belongings, relationships, and habits he keeps. These still reflect him and his ever-evolving sense of consciousness. For others, he must discover a way of being that's more suitable.

One of my clients exemplified the challenges and promises of kundalini during this life period. A father of four, he had married while in his late twenties, while employed by the military. The woman was only twenty-one. She quit school so they could marry and immediately began having babies. He then left the military for a corporate job. The two became pillars of a born-again Christian church, one that touted men as natural and rightful leaders and the women as subservient partners.

In his fifties, the man flung himself into an affair. He wasn't in love with the woman, but he enjoyed the multiple escapes from his life, adding drinking and smoking pot to the sexual fling. Did his kundalini encourage this breakaway? I don't believe so, but the kundalini sure made use of it. Soon after my client began these rendezvous, he began to fall apart, reporting bouts of mania, hot flashes, depression, and suicidal thoughts. His church-based beliefs didn't help; he found no answers in dogma. His wife ignored the problems and pretended everything was normal.

Finally, as he was spinning out of the "safe nest" of systems, correctness, and protocol, he started to unearth his deeper pains and needs, and the kundalini—the Divine—took advantage of the situation. Certainly the Divine doesn't encourage harmful behavior, but it will make use of anything that might encourage us to move closer to our spiritual truth. Working with a therapist and myself, my client tiptoed into his pain, eventually recalling traumatic memories of sexual and physical abuse. He didn't like exploring these issues and his subsequent life choices, but he did it. The pain, once unleashed, wasn't going to abate without real emotional honesty.

As with most catch-up work, the worst part of the process is feeling the feelings—not only the current ones, but also the old and repressed ones. As time went on, my client's heart began to soften. He even started to love himself. He ended his affair, making amends for leading the woman on, and he left his marriage. He started crawling out of the sanitized cocoon he had hid within for so long. At long last, he began to build genuine connections with his children, who at first rejected him for "ruining" their mother's life. As they let him in, they began to reveal their own needs and pains, some buried within their own addictions. Finally, my client entered a relationship—one he termed a spiritual partnership. The exterior of his life now mirrored the interior of his being. My client now describes his life as "real"—because of its beauty and because of his continually emerging capacity to feel for self and others.

When working with younger men, I often notice that they are more willing to feel and stretch than the baby boomer group and older generations. More commonly, I perceive them struggling with how to slip their sensitive, creative, innovative, or emotionally based natures into a world that has not yet expanded to accept them. This brings to mind a particularly engaging young man who attended a seminar I taught at a healing school.

This young man had recently quit college because he didn't fit in. Instead, he was actively cultivating consciousness through yoga and energy medicine. "I'm not here to be like everyone else," he explained passionately, tears leaking from his eyes. When I asked about the sorrow, he explained, "I just don't fit. I've been told my entire life I've bi-something or other or borderline this-and-that, and all I really want to do is help the world."

This young man knew his kundalini was engaged and was thoughtfully engendering a divinely inspired compassion for self and others. His heartfelt misery centered on "how" questions: How was he to be himself? How could he assert his authenticity without sliding off the planet? How could he align with a world that didn't dance to his rhythm? I assured him that the world would accept him; that was why he was here, after all. This relieved him of the pressure of thinking himself too strange to be accepted. I next encouraged him to simply open—open to the people who were able to see him for what he was, an amazing being of light. He began to cultivate friendships with people of all walks and ages, those who shared the desire to make a difference to others. He simultaneously created and founded a community and is now creating an Internet-based platform for networking leaders to share goodness in the world.

I have met many young boys and older men whose kundalini is already pulsing away, compelling an obvious connection to higher consciousness. Many of these boys and men have bolstered my own stretch for the stars.

One such mentor was a seventy-five-year-old shaman, Charles, who lived in New York City and taught healing. His entire apartment was full of red pillows; the color was a testimony to the Mother, his name for the kundalini, whom he had met doing journeying, or shaman soul-flying, in Peru. This gentleman constantly encouraged the development of my own and others' true and creative selves. A would-be writer, I was scared to so much as read a word I'd written or even thought out loud. What did Charles do but sit me down in the middle of a circle of people and tell me to begin storytelling. Quaking and shaking, I did so. The story was good, if I say so myself. What kundalini had done was enthrall and excite my mentor into helping others understand their own greatness despite our hesitation.

Regarding the younger generation, I personally believe that many boys are already full or at least partially aware of their own divine light and could instruct the rest of us. One evening, my girlfriend and I drove my ten-year-old son's friends home from an evening out. These four boys from Catholic school conducted the most amazing conversation, one apparently not uncommon to them. They began by supporting one of the youngsters in accepting his emotional sensitivity, as "even Jesus wept, you know." They continued to insist that he might also look for a different way to "express his consciousness."

As this in-depth and conscientious exploration of truth continued, my friend and I stared at each other with our mouths open. Finally, she asked them if they always talked like this.

"Yes, all of us do," explained one of the youngsters. "Even my Internet friends." A few years before, the then-eight-year-old had started an Internet site for global peace, and children from around the world now participated.

Kundalini is available to boys and men no matter their age. While each age is special, the masculine is special at any age. The primary job for a boy or man experiencing kundalini is to ask the questions that must be asked and to find the answers that are there to be found. These aren't always easy questions or simple answers; they aren't supposed to be. What's important is the search for self—for the self one was, really is, and can be. Kundalini is in the unique position to help with this search because it is female. Without kundalini's unconditional love, we cannot peer inside and find what we want—or don't want—to see. The nature of the feminine is essentially this: the essence of complete, total, and perfect love. By falling into the arms of this unconditional Mother, a man can become the man he really is.

The Man's Path Upward

While a boy or man can be initiated by kundalini at any age, the most common phases for a kundalini leap are puberty, the late twenties to early thirties, and the late forties to early fifties. These are times when the male psyche is naturally seeking change and when the light is clearly illuminated against the dark.

The seventh chakra activates in all children at the age of fourteen. It develops over the next seven years, during which time we recycle the issues lying within our lower chakras and prepare for adulthood. Entering adulthood is a process, one that includes becoming aware of our talents, some of which are spiritual, while facing the need to eventually make a living. As well, we experiment with relationships so as to eventually select one that supports and enlivens our spiritual development. While girls undergo this process as clearly as do boys, the seventh chakra is a male-oriented chakra, and so this phase is especially vibrant and stimulating for boys.

Whereas the first chakra interacts with things of this world, from sex to money to property, the goal of the kundalini is the seventh chakra, a window to the light, the cosmos, and the Divine. If the first chakra enables us to manifest "everything," the seventh chakra mitigates the goal by saying, "Everything is about nothing. What counts is what lasts." Pubescent boys are simultaneously encompassed in this highly spiritual, masculine energy and throbbing with the very real physical hormones that stimulate their first chakras. The distance between the first and the seventh chakras—the body and the spirit—can seem unsurmountable, even too far to jump. Sometimes the stretch between the two can stimulate a kundalini awakening; sometimes the addictions, drugs, sexual experiences, or even fears related to this chasm can do the same. And sometimes the spirit pulls the kundalini upward, and a boy becomes a man not because he has to, but because he gracefully matures into it.

The second most active kundalini phase for males is the late twenties. In my twelve-chakra system, both men and women are actively engaged in the ruminations of the eighth chakra between ages twenty-one and twenty-eight. These can be tough years, as they pull up issues related to past lives, karma, and our shadow, or hidden, traits. When we reach twenty-eight, the divine sage within us all rings the bell and invites us into the haven of the ninth chakra, the golden land of spiritual purpose and harmony. A masculine chakra, the ninth is particularly powerful for men, for it provides a clear contrast between the temptations of the modern age and the summons of the heart. Ultimately, men stand at this portal and must respond to the following question, which will determine the course of his life and also his interaction with the kundalini: *What service are you here to provide?*

On one side of him, a teleprompter, with these types of answers: *Making money. Having a lot of sex. Becoming famous. Being like everyone else.*

On the other side, a blank slate and a pencil, inviting him to write or draw his own answer to that question by drawing upon his inner wisdom.

If he is willing to leap into the void, kundalini immediately activates, rising up to lift him into the heavens and to also help set his feet on the earth so he may walk it in a good way. These risings are seldom hard, fast, or dangerous. Rather, they are kind, supportive, and lenient.

The last of the most common kundalini activations occurs during the so-called midlife crisis years, which we explored earlier in this chapter. Most typically, a man has either erected the life he was expected to build or has fallen short of his dreams. At this point, kundalini—sometimes furtively, sometimes passionately—enters into the picture, showcasing the unknown so that a man might become everything he can be, not only a part of himself.

At any time, kundalini can be confusing and confounding. There is a concept in the Eastern world, however, that lights a path through the male awakening process. It is the way of the spiritual warrior; the addition of spirit, the energy of the seventh chakra, to the warrior, the power of the first chakra.

To merge spirit with the warrior is to embody one's spirit in the physical temple of the body. What is the nature of the spiritual warrior? In the words of Rick Field, author of *The Code of the Warrior*, true warriors have a mission beyond themselves. They do not simply focus on day-to-day events, nor do they hyperfocus on long-range goals. Rather, they live in the middle. They develop their mission and a set of values that can be applied in real life.[72]

Following are exercises designed to help men, and the masculine within us all, embrace and fully embody the best of the kundalini process.

EXERCISES

Healing a Man's Heart

There are two breathing practices that energize both the first and the seventh chakras, encouraging them to conjoin in the heart, the center of spiritual warriorism. These exercises can be done one right after the other or separately.

Long, deep breathing is a great way to relax and recover from the stress of societal and internal expectations. It can help you become aware of the movement of your diaphragm and is a good precursor to the second breathing exercise, the breath of fire. The breath of fire cleanses and energizes. It charges the nervous system and releases sexual hormones into the bloodstream. While these hormones include testosterone, which can increase libido and passion, there are other hormones, including oxytocin, which promotes bonding and love. These encourage the link between spirit and body, feminine and masculine, both inside and outside of the self. The nature of these and other hormones is explored in the next chapter. If used over time and with a variety of yogic practices, the breath of fire can help balance magnetic and electrical energies, clear the mind, and increase radiance, making it easier to attract what you need to yourself without stress and force. The aim is to grow into the heart space, where the "I am" lives.

(1) Long, Deep Breathing

Sit cross-legged and take a long, deep breath. As you inhale, press the air into the lower part of your body, filling your abdominal area. Arch forward slightly with your palms on your knees. Now, with your arms straight, press your palms against your knees—inward, toward your lower body. You should feel your chest cavity, including the upper lungs, open forward without needing to open your rib cage or raise your shoulders.

Your lungs filled, hold your breath for a moment and press your shoulders back. Expand your chest so you can feel the full length of your diaphragm. Now contract the entire length of the diaphragm, from the upper chest to the abdomen, squeezing out all the air.

(2) Breath of Fire

Once you have mastered the diaphragmatic long, deep breathing, you can energize yourself with the breath of fire. This exercise involves pulling in air and pumping it out rhythmically, like a bellows, with no tension in your upper body.

Start with the long, deep breathing. When your lungs are completely expanded, force the air out. When it is out, pull air back in. Each time, arch your spine forward and press your palms lightly, inward against your knees. You should feel your diaphragm fill your lungs from back to front, then contract again. Start breathing faster until a rhythm takes over.[73]

The Kundalini of Coupledom

Piglet sidled up to Pooh from behind. "Pooh!" he whispered. "Yes, Piglet?" "Nothing," said Piglet, taking Pooh's paw. "I just wanted to be sure of you."

—A. A. Milne, *Winnie-the-Pooh*

We all long to wake up in the morning with that special someone at our side. We'd really like it if our significant other would serve us coffee in bed, but we'll take a smile instead.

Depending on how a couple—same sex or different—utilizes kundalini, a kundalini-based connection between two individuals promises beautiful results. In this chapter, we explore the power of kundalini to create oneness where there was once twoness, delving deliciously into the concepts of Tantra to explore the keys to intimacy. Along the way, we'll stop at the other extreme, that of biology, showcasing exactly what happens in the body when two try to become one. At the end of the chapter, there's play—exercises for solo and joined practice. And yes, we'll discuss sex.

chapter eleven

Kundalini:
The Hormonal Engine

There's a reason why kundalini is so often linked to sex. As it rises, it activates the sexual hormones, part of the engine that makes a man a man and a woman a woman.

As explored in chapter 5, the kundalini interfaces with all of our hormones. Each chakra links with a different endocrine gland, which means that the rising kundalini fire does more than blow smoke. It ignites our hormones and, in doing so, promotes unification inside of us. The relationship between kundalini and the sexual hormones, however, is unique. It could be pictured in the same way as the kundalini is often portrayed: a snake swallowing its own tail. Kundalini ignites the sex hormones, and increased sex hormones stimulate the kundalini.

Testosterone is the primary male sexual hormone. Too much can result in mania and crazy behavior. Not enough, and men and women alike suffer a lack of stamina. What is one of the most important determinants of a healthy testosterone level? Stress management. Too much stress—or the inability to manage it—accounts for most problematic testosterone fluctuations.

Estrogen is the primary female sexual hormone. It is counter-balanced by progesterone, which wanes as it waxes, and vice versa. Estrogen enflames and empowers, while progesterone calms and soothes. Kundalini seems to increase as the estrogen peaks and decreases as progesterone ebbs. Kundalini can, therefore, be seen as a bit of a troublemaker. Its relationship with these ovarian-based hormones emphasizes the importance of the second chakra in a women's shift into enlightenment.[74]

Kundalini encourages healthy hormone balance within individuals of both genders. It does so as part of the enlightenment cycle, which could be compared to a romantic relationship. Consider what happens inside of the body when we fall in love.

Kundalini Falls in Love

Research shows that testosterone, present in both men and women, kicks off infatuation, creating desire for a wild sexual splurge. During the next stage, that of romance and obsession, the body generates the stimulants dopamine and norepinephrine, coupled with low levels of serotonin. As a couple enters the attachment stage, the peaceful part of a long-term relationship, their bodies now produce oxytocin and vasopressin, often called the love hormones. These hormones are produced not only in the brain but also the heart, implying that kundalini is especially in favor of heart-based, intimate relationships—relationships both with ourselves and between ourselves and others.

The hormonal changes triggered by a kundalini awakening may very well mirror the hormonal shifts of a growing love relationship. It is possible that testosterone serves as the predominant agent during the kindling phase of a kundalini awakening, encouraging a sexual heat. When rising, kundalini next throws its subject into a shock and transmutation phase, activating dopamine and norepinephrine. Next is the (hopefully) smooth slide into peace and enlightenment, a substantiation stage spurred on by vasopressin and oxytocin. These two hormones are the same ones, by the way, that underlie a blissful orgasm. The goal of kundalini could, therefore, be likened to a sustained orgasm of peace and calm.[75]

As a matchmaker, kundalini often lights the fire of a relationship. What it does inside of our body—fanning the flame inside—it also does between us and another. In that Shakti clears a pathway to her spiritual consort, Shiva, so does she offer the same service in a relationship by inviting union, bliss, and attachment. In short, kundalini creates better relationships, and better relationships nurture the kundalini.

Tips for securing this type of relationship can be found in Tantra, the branch of yoga famous for lighting paths to intimacy. To deepen our exploration of coupledom, let's turn to Tantra and see what it might say.

Tempted by Tantra, Anyone?

Okay, we're finally there: *sex*.

In Western culture, the term *Tantric sex* is has become a synonym for free sex, sexual conquests, and sexual plunder. In some minds, the entire reason for inducing or desiring a kundalini rising is to enjoy these sexual pleasures. Some people practice certain versions of Tantric sex in order to trigger a kundalini awakening, just so they can enjoy more sex.

Sex is great. Sex is lovely and pleasurable, bonding and exciting. It is also only one facet of a real relationship and of the kundalini.

There are three main types of Tantra in regard to sexuality, although only two of these are well known.[76] According to Yogi Bhajan, a well-known contemporary Tantric master, Red Tantric Yoga directs energy for sexual purposes. This type of Tantra usually requires or recommends sexual intercourse as a path for spiritual development. It is easy to see how this Tantric approach can be misused, its practitioners convincing themselves they are actually developing their kundalini when they are really going for sex. Sex alone does not create intimacy. True intimacy occurs when both partners are fully awakened and/or assisting each other with their individual awakenings. We receive the full benefit of a coupling only when all our chakras are connected internally and with those of another.

Practicing sex simply for the orgasmic effects is not the goal of kundalini-based sexual practices. Relationships cultivated strictly for sexual purposes fail to develop a man beyond his first chakra. Women get tired of placating a man's first chakra. Based in the second chakra, a woman will attempt to lift a relationship to the emotional level. But relationships must also move beyond the second chakra, or emotional interconnectedness, to be fully realized.

White Tantric Yoga emphasizes the joining of male and female energies. This joining can be done within the self, as promoted through the concept of the feminine kundalini rising to meet her male consort. White Tantric Yoga also allows the merging of male and female energies between two loving partners. One of the practices of White Tantric Yoga involves the creation of intimacy between couples. Some of these processes are conducted in group settings; the two members of a couple face each other—with their clothes on; there is no sexual intercourse or sexual activity of any sort. But there is connection, and through this connection is the clearing of karma, old issues, and resistance to enlightenment.

A third type of Tantra, called Black Tantra, encourages the manipulation of another human being through energetic means. This type of Tantra is not enlightening.[77]

Just to clarify: not everyone who practices Tantra involves him- or herself in sexual matters. Many Tantric practitioners apply the concepts toward personal development and to perform higher service, sometimes choosing to be celibate for a certain amount of time or for the rest of their lives. All forms of Tantra, however, encourage the full acceptance of both the feminine and masculine and the embodiment of the two.

Chakra-Based Intimacy

We are able to foster intimacy between the feminine and masculine aspects of ourselves, as well as with a partner, with various chakra-based activities. When we share certain activities as a couple, in fact, we actually open and expand the related chakra. Healthier chakras enable a clear passage for our individual kundalini energies, and they also help us share kundalini energy with our partner. Remember that kundalini is essentially a divine energy. Energy can pass through barriers, including our skin. To share the light of our divinity with another is to unify us both with the Divine. Intimacy now leads to the merging of two selves with the Divine, forming a magical trinity of interconnection. Now all things are possible.

Chakra-based activities that increase intimacy and the expansion of kundalini include the following:

First chakra: Physical, including sexual, activities, but also shared physical interests such as sports, hobbies, and running a household.

Second chakra: Emotional activities, including creative endeavors such as taking art classes.

Third chakra: Mental activities, including shared intellectual interests, supporting each other's work, and scheduling time together.

Fourth chakra: Relational activities, including those done independent of each other, those done as a couple, those done with loved ones, and those with the Divine. Supporting each other's personal healing processes is a relational activity.

Fifth chakra: Communication, speaking and listening to each other, as well as living by similar higher principles.

Sixth chakra: Vision, working together toward long-range goals.

Seventh chakra: Spiritual activities such as living by shared values and ultimately cocreating a spiritual mission together.

Eighth chakra: Mystical relating, such as a common interest in mystical pursuits and supporting each other to heal karma and awaken repressed spiritual gifts.

Ninth chakra: Global relating, or a shared desire to create peace and to have a positive effect on the greater world.

Tenth chakra: Natural concerns, such as a shared commitment to sustainability and caring for nature.

Eleventh chakra: Commanding or working as a couple, rather than just two solo people, to effect the healing of the world.

Twelfth chakra: Supporting each other's attainment of individual mastery.

Into You, Into Me—
Using Kundalini-Based Practices to Build Intimacy

This is the first of four exercises in this chapter that are designed to encourage true and complete intimacy between two people—intimacy that includes, but is not limited to, sexual gratification. Intimacy means "into you, into me." It involves the formation of a third entity—the relationship.

As hinted in the previous section, where two are gathered, there is God. The Divine flows through each individual, pulsing our kundalini toward an even higher light, but it seeks always to connect. Relationships are a fusion of the feminine, the masculine, and the Divine. They are an alchemical mix of delight and love, light and truth. We don't have sex to cultivate the kundalini; we don't even cultivate the kundalini to have better sex. We seek to unify the human and divine elements of ourselves with the same in someone else in order to experience and, eventually, even become love. Spiritual partnerships, those that enfold the kundalini into a higher and loving goal, create more love for everyone to share.

The outlined practices are adapted from various kundalini yoga or White Tantric Yoga ideas and can be conducted in a safe, monogamous, committed relationship, one you would like to develop and nurture. Enjoy!

Starting Solo: *The Floating Exercise (Loving Your Body)*

Before we can enjoy the heart, mind, soul, or body of another person, we must like our own body. In other words, all intimacy starts inside of the self. You cannot give yourself to someone else if you cannot first love and be comfortable with yourself.

Many individuals dislike their bodies, internalizing society's rigid views of physical perfection. If you are a woman, know that you have a beautiful, lovely, feminine body, no matter what it looks like, no matter if you are having a bad hair day or even a bad hair year. If you are a man, embrace the masculine, sensitive strength of your body, no matter how in or out of shape you are. For both men and women, know that to acknowledge your body is to name it as its own. You are then able enjoy another person's body.

This is not a sexual exercise. You perform it entirely alone. Its only goal is to help you love, own, and trust yourself.

This exercise is a synopsis of one designed by Reverend David Howell. You can read the full version on the website the Global Oneness Commitment (www.experiencefestival.com).

Before starting, find a quiet, secure location and become comfortable. You need about an hour of undisturbed silence. If you want, you can be naked or take off clothing to your own comfort. *You are alone and safe.* Make sure you have enough blankets and pillows to stay warm.

Now relax each muscle in your body, step by step, slowing your breathing from the usual twelve to fourteen breaths per minute to about four breaths per minute, if possible. Do this by counting slowly to seven as you breathe out and again to seven slowly as you breathe in. Do not stop and hold your breath. As soon as you have filled your lungs with air, immediately breathe out. Do not push the air; instead, allow it to move smoothly. Take in extra air if you need to. This breathing technique is a pranayama method and should be continued for about twelve minutes.

Now imagine you are a raft that is floating on a river. Lying on the raft (nude, if you choose), you are totally isolated and safe. You can see everything around you. No one can intrude. This is a haven of safety and security.

You notice everything about this river. There are birds and butterflies, fish and sweet breezes. The weather is perfect, the sky blue with fluffy clouds. The shore is replete with lush green grasses and beautiful pine trees. Low mountains rise in the distance. You see a few sandy beaches along the calm shores. Everything around you is kind; nothing and no one is creating pain for another.

The raft itself is a perfect design for your personality. It might be logs tied together with ropes or a Nile River raft. No matter what type of raft it is, you are completely secure and at peace.

You only need to float on the raft and enjoy the scenery. You are enjoying your own creation and the divinity within the self that has created a pleasurable, safe experience. When you want to, direct the raft to one of the sandy beaches, get out, and enjoy the sun or walk the beach. Then return to your raft to continue floating.

When done with your journey, return to the here and now. This river is your own special place; it is a safe and boundaried setting for your own enjoyment alone. You have created it and can return anytime you want, never with anyone else—not a partner, friend, or guru. Know that no one can pressure you to become what you are not, not for any reason. It is safe to be you and alone.

The Seven Rights and a Rite for Truth

One of the goals of a relationship is to heal our inner wounds. A true kundalini process not only supports but also relies on self-healing. Our inner injuries are most often caused by the failure to embrace our basic rights, usually because we weren't treated with respect when growing up, or even since then. Healing is even more powerful when conducted between two loving individuals.

Each of the seven basic chakras reflects a basic right. To understand these rights is to support our self as an individual, to make positive choices, and to attract beneficial situations, including love in a relationship. If we were treated unfairly when we were growing up or since becoming an adult, we may not know that we have these rights.

For instance, if we were sexually violated, a type of abuse that imprints in the first chakra, we might not understand we deserve the right to be safe. If our feelings were constantly ignored or criticized, we might not know that we deserve to be heard or cared about. We will shut down our second chakra and be unable to fully embrace the basic right inherent within it.

Following is an outline of the rights inherent in each chakra, based on my own work and the footnoted source.[78]

Chakra	Right	Symptoms or Problems
First	To exist and have what we need	Survival threatened, needs unmet. *Fear forces energy into higher chakras.*
Second	To feel, understand, have wants and needs	Not cared about, discount self. *Guilt makes us hide true self.*
Third	To act, to be innovative and free	Stuck, contained, controlled. *Shame hinders self-esteem.*
Fourth	To love and be loved	Unlovability, loneliness. *Grief blocks love.*
Fifth	To speak and hear truth	Not listened to, secrets, dishonesty. *Lies blur our relationship to world.*

Sixth	To see	Told we're wrong, vision denied. *Illusion confuses our perception.*
Seventh	To know truth and spiritual knowledge	Denied the right to be our divine self, to know God. *Attachment obscures our spirit.*

Do any of these symptoms or problems seem familiar? During a kundalini rising, the issues that are keeping us from embracing our rights come forward. While it is vitally important to address these issues personally, it is extremely helpful to express and heal them through a relationship. In fact, relationships often stir up our innate issues, causing us to question our rights. Why not turn to your partner to help you transform yourself and your partner, and create a whole and happy relationship?

You can use the following exercise to help yourself and your partner embrace the truth: you have a right to your rights.

EXERCISE

Right to Rights

To begin, sit in an easy pose, back to back, spines together. Deeply inhale and exhale, then begin in unison to chant *Sa-Ta-Na-Ma* for five minutes.

You are now going to focus on each chakra, one at a time. While focused on a chakra, repeat the statement correlating to each chakra seven times, in each of these four ways:

- At the same time, out loud
- Whispering, at the same time
- To each other, one at a time
- At the same time, out loud

The phrases for each chakra are:

First: I own the right to exist. (When speaking to the other person, you will say, "I acknowledge your right to exist.")

Second: I own the right to my needs. (To the other, you will say, "I acknowledge your right to your needs.")

Third: I own the right to freely act. (To the other, you will say, "I acknowledge your right to act freely.")

Fourth: I own the right to love and be loved. (To the other, you will say, "I acknowledge your right to love and be loved.")

Fifth: I own the right to speak and hear truth. (To the other, you will say, "I acknowledge your right to speak and hear truth.")

Sixth: I own the right to see. (To the other, you will say, "I acknowledge your right to see.")

Seventh: I own the right to spiritual truth. (To the other, you will say, "I acknowledge your right to spiritual truth.")

Complete the exercise by chanting *Sa-Ta-Na-Ma* for a couple more minutes and then end with a hug.

EXERCISE

Channeling Sexual Energy: *The Great Lock*

There are times in all of our lives that we need to redirect our sexual energy toward nonsexual pursuits. Perhaps we need to manage an intense kundalini experience and not fritter it away on undesirable sex. Maybe we need to heal prior sexual abuse issues, we are not currently in a relationship, or we have chosen to remain celibate for a time.

The root lock, or mul bandh, introduced in chapter 6, helps redirect sexual energy toward creative and healing endeavors. The other option for redirecting sexual energy is to combine all three bhandas, or body locks—the neck, diaphragm, and root locks (also covered in chapter 6)—into what has called the great lock, or *maha bandh*. By working with all three body locks at the same time, you can relieve a preoccupation with sex. The great lock also helps circulate blood into the reproductive glands and tones male and female sexual organs.[79]

To do the great lock, start with the root lock, add the diaphragm lock, and then the neck lock. The neck lock should be applied at the end of a deep exhalation and released on the inhalation immediately after.

Here are more detailed directions for the great lock:

First the root lock: As you exhale, contract the anal muscle, drawing it in and up. Add a contraction similar to that felt in orgasm. Now draw your lower abdomen toward your spine, pulling in your navel and drawing up your rectum and sexual organs. This lock is usually applied at the end of a deep exhalation and released on the next inhalation. During the inhalation, sense energy moving up your spine and end the in-breath by focusing on your sixth or seventh chakras.

Now the diaphragm lock: Only on the exhalation, pull your upper abdomen muscles backward, toward your spine, and lift your diaphragm into your chest.

Finally the neck lock: At the end of a deep exhalation, contract your neck and throat with your head level.

You are now performing the great lock, which is released at the next inhalation.

Yoga for Couples:
Looking into the Heart

From a yoga viewpoint, a committed relationship carries us into the infinite. Our partner mirrors our best and worst qualities, and vice versa.

To unify as one spirit in two bodies mirrors the ultimate goal of a kundalini rising, the unification of Shakti and Shiva. As we grow to accept our partner, we embrace parts of ourselves. When we give, we also receive. Especially in an opposite-sex relationship, this sharing helps us blend the polar energies within ourselves.

Following is a yoga exercise that can be used to create oneness between yourself and your partner.

Sit in a comfortable position across from each other so that your knees are almost touching. Position yourselves so that you can easily and comfortably look into each other's eyes. (Use pillows to raise yourself up, if needed.) Form your hands into a lotus flower by putting the base of your hands and wrists together and then spreading your hands and fingers to form a cup. Your little fingers will be near each other. The man (or partner taking this role) will put his little fingers under the woman's. Only these fingers touch as you look into your partner's eyes, seeking to embrace his or her heart and soul. Maintain this position and gaze for one and a half minutes.

Put one hand over the other on your heart. Close your eyes. Meditate on your heart, traveling deep into your core self. Spend a minute and a half doing this. Now inhale deeply and exhale three times. Relax and thank your partner.[80]

Kundalini and Spirituality

And through this citadel walk graceful men and women with lovely elongated faces and calm, knowing eyes—with a glint of mischief—and they are perfect and know it and they are imperfect and know it.

—Freda Warrington, *Elfland*

chapter twelve

I received the frantic call near midnight. "My son is speaking another language!" the woman cried. "His hands are so hot, I can't even hold them."

This mother went on to explain that her son had awoken the day before and told her that a "man full of light" had come into his room and touched his heart. Since then, the ten-year-old had been insisting that there was more to life than his parents could see and that if we could but see the light around, we'd all love each other. To prove his point, the child had placed his burning hands on his mother's heart, and her long-standing arrhythmia had disappeared.

I believe that this child had experienced a true mystical moment, which could be called a sudden awakening of his kundalini. The kundalini leaped

225

so high, he achieved near-instant wisdom. After encouraging the mother to take the appropriate medical steps, I suggested a few readings about kundalini, enlightenment, and mysticism. She became less frightened and called back a few days later to report that the child's enlightenment experience, for it was truly that, had faded. The heat cooled; he remembered his English. But something remained different about him, his mother told me. "He has a kindness that simply radiates from him."

This child was able to quicken from "normal" to "sage" with an immediacy few of us experience. In many ways, however, his path is just beginning. The spiritual is about living fully in the spirit—the keyword being *living*.

Kundalini as a Stairway to the Divine

Kundalini is more than a metaphor for a rush along our nervous system. It is not a pretext for animism or spiritism or an excuse for out-of-control behavior. All kundalini-based practices are aimed at filling us with the spirit that is already present. Dynamic and evolving, they stair-step us to enlightenment; our job is to walk up the ladder. Regardless which branch of yoga or kundalini practice you explore, the message is the same: there is a higher goal, and that higher goal is to live as your highest self. Kundalini is an energetic staircase that, if climbed, leads to one place and one place alone: the Divine.

A contemporary expert on yoga, B. K. S. Iyengar, puts it this way: The aim of yoga is true union with God. All practices and disciplines should "yoke" the parts of us to bring our soul into the position of peering evenly at all aspects of life.

This is the teaching of mystics across time. Yogic and Tantric practices are entirely based on the awakening of kundalini energy, the raw Shakti power latent within each of us. This force can be initiated by a guru or compelled by disciplines, including breath

Kundalini in Christianity, Islam, and Judaism

Three major world religions each include a story of kundalini energy, although they call it by a different name.

Salaat is the kundalini yoga of Islam. Many branches of Islam overlook the feminine qualities of God. Salaat, in contrast, acknowledges that ancient Arabs believed that Allah had a counterpart. Her name is *Al-Lat*, a name considered to be the same as Salaat. Her name is a reference to the burning, or serpentine, fire that activates a solar force in the spine. As with other forms of yoga, this serpent power is feminine. As with other forms of kundalini yoga, the goal of the Salaat yoga process involves helping the serpent power rise between the first chakra and the seventh through the nadis, thus activating the path of enlightenment. In raising this fire, Salaat yoga employs asanas, or postures, similar to those of traditional Yoga. It also recommends a set of purification processes comparable to those of Christian traditions, including the laying on of hands and foot washing.[81]

In the original language of the Christian Old Testament, as in the Jewish Torah, the word for "Holy Spirit" is feminine. The flames that appeared over the heads of Jesus's followers at the first Pentecost are considered a feminine fire. Later, secret Christian brotherhoods, such as the Masons, spoke of a spirit fire that rises through the spinal column.[82]

In all three traditions—Islam, Judaism, and Christianity—humans are believed to have been created out of red dirt or clay. This signifies the formation of the physical body out of fire. The first man, like the first syllable of the sacred name of Jehovah, was Yod, which represents the Flame, the Cause, the One on which all things are based. The second letter of God's name is He, which is feminine. From these come Vau, or son, and in last place syllabically, a final He, or daughter. Thus, we find in the earliest roots of all three major religions the story of the male and female aspects of God and ourselves.[83]

control, physical exercises, visualizations, and chanting. It can flip on overnight; it can even be gifted by a spirit. No matter what the initiation method is, the kundalini energy slides up the spine and the initiate begins to feel differently.

On each rung toward divinity, with each increment of kundalini energy, we face the demons of our fears. To avoid pain, we might be tempted to stop the ascent of energy, to lose ourselves in confusion and to fall into licentious practices. In the end, as we continue to strive, the challenges we face bring us into oneness with the Divine. We attain higher consciousness through the merging of our feminine energy with our masculine energy, our physical self with our divine self. We enjoy divine wisdom, self-realization, gnosis, self-knowledge, pure joy, pure knowledge, and pure love.[84]

Attaining this spiritual reality is a possibility open to all of us. This was the teaching of the *rishis*, or wise ones, who first brought us knowledge of the kundalini. This is the teaching of the well-known contemporary guru Gopi Krishna, who described his spontaneous kundalini awakening this way: "Suddenly, with a roar like that of a waterfall, I felt a stream of liquid light entering my brain through the spinal cord…I was now all consciousness without any outline…immersed in a sea of light, simultaneously conscious and aware at every point."[85]

Further describing himself as a vast circle of consciousnesses, his body a prick within it, Gopi Krishna experienced extreme exultation and happiness. He came to believe that kundalini energy underlies most of the religions originating with personal revelation. He also understood that this aspiration for consciousness was physical in orientation, originating in the brain, in the region called *Brahma-Randhra* in the yogic tradition—possibly the pineal gland.[86]

Personal Enlightenment Leads to Global Enlightenment

Gopi Krishna recognized the enormous potential of kundalini energy. He noted its connection to sex and materialism, the energy of the first chakra, and that because of our compulsive nature, humankind can and has used the kundalini force for harmful ends. But he also understood that kundalini energy must be awakened, and not only for one's personal attainment of bliss. It is also a necessary ingredient for human and planetary evolution.

As Krishna expressed it, nature's higher law is evolution. Each of us must personally safeguard our kundalini awakening, applying principles such as decorum, morality, and discipline in order to orient the kundalini toward the advancement of consciousness. Toward this end, he advocated sex within a loving relationship, diet control, practical work, and other methods for living a normal life. Collectively, we must harness the kundalini power to become a better people.[87] Though Gopi Krishna's advice doesn't officially mirror the ten living principles discussed in chapter 8, they are similar. To follow the principles of life is to flow with our kundalini, and to lovingly flow with our kundalini is to embrace the divine life.

Gopi Krishna invites a solid, grounded approach to kundalini, one that complements spirituality with practicality. By doing so, he enforces two Hindu principles: karma and dharma.

Karma and Dharma

A lot of people ask me what karma means. The common thought is that it is a law of judgment. If I injure someone, the same will be done unto me. Conversely, if I've been really good, I'll reap a reward.

This simplistic notion doesn't make sense. Take a look at victims of childhood abuse. They did nothing wrong. Yet studies show that survivors of such suffering live painful lives, physically, emotionally, and relationally. If there were some grand way for the score to be evened, wouldn't their lives be better instead of worse? We've only to examine the list of the rich and famous to figure out that money can equate to the "Get Out of Jail Free" card from the Monopoly game—or perhaps one better, a "Never Go to Jail" card.

I've discovered that karma is a much richer and a more loving principle than one of cause and effect. Enlightenment is the assumption of forgiveness and restoration. This means that karma is a tool for learning, but it is also a healing process, a way to evolve into the perfection that we are. In fact, on the Vedic path, karma means action. We pursue yoga and other kundalini pursuits so that our actions match our goals. If we desire union with the Divine, then we must adopt the disciplined behavior necessary to attain that oneness.

Bliss and enlightenment are worthy, desirable goals, but it can be difficult to take the action steps to achieve these. Whatever our distractions, be they a plate of cookies or a sexual fling, these off-path activities earn us a reaction from the universe. We gain weight. We lose our spouse. We become more unhappy and further away from the ultimate goal of unity.

Karma does not punish; it could be termed consequences. We act, and then there are consequences, good or bad. This process could seem like a neverending loop, and it would be if we never grew and changed. Teacher Ravi Ravindra states the law of karma as this:

"As one acts, so one becomes; as one is, so one acts."[88]

One of the ways I employ the gift of karma is to ask for universal feedback for my behavior. If I err, I don't want to wait five years or a lifetime to make a correction and express my true, more loving self. So I play an instant karma game. In other words, if I make a mistake, I want to know about it immediately.

The approach works. One day I threw a newspaper into a public garbage can—and missed. Feeling lazy and overwhelmed with a baby in diapers, I pretended I hadn't noticed. The next day I found a heap of garbage on my lawn. I cleaned it up, smiling. I actually felt loved; the Divine cared enough about me to nudge me to improve. I now think more often before I act.

The key to the karma game is to abstain from shame, the energy that insists that if you do something wrong, *you* are wrong. Healthy guilt simply says, "This isn't you. You can change." It's actually an empowering emotion and a call to evolution.

Within the law of karma is the whisper of evolution. If we act with integrity, we become a better person, and it is easier to be kind and loving. Progress takes nothing more than an active commitment to evolution.

In yoga, kundalini energy is like an escalator that moves us toward a singular goal, the transformation from our natural form to a perfected form. The word for our natural or vulgar state is *prakriti* in Sanskrit. When in this state, we repeat actions that keep us stuck, unable to flow with our kundalini. Even if the kundalini is activating our spiritual awareness, our visions will get confused with human-induced fantasies. Through a disciplined approach to kundalini, we become *sanskrita*, or "well made."[89]

If karma is the principle that makes us look at our actions to determine if they are freeing us from prison walls or entrapping us, then dharma is the other side of the coin, the reason we self-examine and evolve personally. If karma calls us to act in alignment with our spirit, dharma shines the light on our spirit.

Dharma means "obligations." This concept acknowledges the need to operate within a set of personal duties and responsibilities. When we do this, we sustain the cosmic order and evolve into our greater self.[90]

As dry as this definition sounds, if it were opened like a coffee-table book, beautiful images appear. Dharma infers that we are here on this planet at this time for a higher purpose. We are needed. We are important. Only you can gift this world in the way unique to you. Kundalini energizes this central purpose, ultimately lifting us into a state of personal freedom, or *moksha*.[91] Paradoxically, the person who has secured perfect freedom is the person that understands the holiness and joy of blending love and selfless duty within the mortal body. This freedom breaks the constraints of maya, the illusion that we are separate from the Divine. We do not become less than who we are; we can simply be more of who we are, more often—in and through everyday life, not in spite of it. As shared by Ken Wilber, an author, deep thinker, and modern mystic, "The awakened Sage is not merely a unique oddity, living alone in a cave in India or perched on a mountain top in Tibet. The awakened Sage—or simply awakened Human—is actually the nature of our very own consciousness, even here and now."[92]

Kundalini's Invitation to Experience the Now

Sometimes we work so hard to grasp enlightenment, we don't see it's snuck up on us from behind. Sometimes we get so caught up in wanting to awaken our kundalini, we don't realize it already has woken up and is at work in our lives. Sometimes we are looking so hard for the dramatic, mind-blowing effects of kundalini, we don't notice the subtle yet profound ways it is moving within us and opening us up.

If enlightenment ever seems far away, or you want to experience the magic of you in this moment, stop and breathe. Let enlightenment catch up with you. Being present is the key to right action and acceptance of purpose.

EXERCISE

Being Present
Try this exercise any time you are feeling guilty about the past, which interferes with the truth of karma, or scared about your future, a resistance to your dharma.

Stand and breathe naturally. Notice the *is*-ness of this moment. Now inhale, exhale, and inhale. Put your palms together at your heart and then cross your hands over your chest. Finally, on a last exhalation, open both hands on either side of your body, and think this: *I breathe out and release to infinity.*

Become the infinite in the finite. Now carry on with your day.

The Carriers of the Kundalini

While I was writing this book, an image kept coming to my mind.

Lines and lines of people encircle me. Their backgrounds are diverse; I know this by their clothing. There are pantaloons from the Renaissance, robes from the Middle East, flamenco swirls of color across cultures and various times. A few figures shine with otherworldly light; others are covered with dust from working the land. Some cry, others laugh; there are those who speak holy words from texts, others who share from their hearts.

No two visitors are alike, but I know that each carries an understanding of—and perhaps a dream for—kundalini, the life force that magnifies our physical existence and awakens us to the higher planes. As I watch, I become excited, waiting to see which figure will separate from the crowd and teach me.

The first to do so is a woman clothed in bright red, her bare feet lined with veins and dirt. Her arms embrace a basket that barely stirs atop her head, although she jogs up a craggy Andean mountain. Kundalini empowers her climb; it enables the

235

feeding of her people. At the summit, she swings the basket to her feet and raises her face to the sun. She receives its blessings. The kundalini has completed its circuit from earth to sky. In that moment, the Andean woman—one of many kundalini teachers—knows herself as whole.

In my mind's eye, the woman smiles and then retreats into the backdrop. Next to move forward is an elderly man, sparkling with a golden light. Levitating in a yogic pose, he leans forward and unrolls a scroll. He grins as I watch a hologram that comes alive, transforming from a sketch into a movie. Here is a human body, the chakras and nadis, not the liver or other physical systems, highlighted within it. A red blaze slowly arises, igniting each of the centers as it moves upward from the base, until it joins a white fire at the top of the head. The subsequent explosion of bliss could light the entirety of the universe. The light dims, but it does not disappear. Instead, it is replaced by a fine glow that illuminates the entire body. This man teaches the more traditional form of kundalini.

I have met many representatives of this crowd of kundalini "informers." Each has presented a slightly different view of kundalini, a particular way to activate, awaken, and express its organic power. There is the housewife who demonstrates how the kundalini helps her to vacuum, the pastor who calls upon kundalini in Holy Spirit form to gift her sermons. There is a man in therapy; he draws upon kundalini to heal the very issues that it triggers. There is the accountant who meditates daily in order to gain wisdom to better serve his clients. Are any of these individuals using kundalini more appropriately than the others? Are any of them right? More inspired than the others?

I don't believe so. In fact, if I were to summarize the real message of this book, it would be that we are all already enlightened. We are already invested with the highest level of feminine power and the equivalent masculine counterpart. We are already "in bliss," already serving a higher spiritual mission and at one with all beings around us. We are simply struggling to remember this truth.

Of course, much of the information in this book has been culled by research—the reading of scriptures, yogic practicums, the Internet—and my own experience. It has come through study, travel, and trial and error. It has not really appeared through mystical contact with spiritual beings across time. Then again, maybe it has. Central to any exploration of kundalini, however, is the story of kundalini in people's lives—in *your* life.

The most important teaching of kundalini lies there, in your own story—in the story of your past, your living in the present, and the hopes for your future. Take a few moments and ask to see your own true self emerge from this crowd of teachers that has instructed me so well and kindly. What would you add to a book like this about kundalini? What would you tell yourself about how to proceed—how to reap, to sow, and to live as the enlightened sage that you are?

Know that you are already empowered to become this informed self. Do so in good health, walking forward in beauty and grace.

As expressed through this Navajo Prayer Song, found by author Leland Waldrip at the Anasazi Museum at Chaco Canyon, New Mexico:

> *Today I will walk out, today everything evil will leave me,*
> *I will be as I was before,*
> *I will have a cool breeze over my body.*
> *I will have a light body,*
> *I will be happy forever, nothing will hinder me.*
> *I walk with beauty before me.*
> *I walk with beauty behind me.*
> *I walk with beauty below me.*
> *I walk with beauty above me.*
> *I walk with beauty around me.*
> *My words will be beautiful.*
> *In beauty all day long may I walk.*

Through the returning seasons, may I walk.
On the trail marked with pollen may I walk.
With dew about my feet may I walk.
With beauty before me may I walk.
With beauty behind me may I walk.
With beauty below me may I walk.
With beauty above me may I walk.
With beauty all around me may I walk.
In old age wandering on a trail of beauty, lively, may I walk.
In old age wandering on a trail of beauty, living again, may I walk.
My words will be beautiful.[93]

This is a list of words found in this book and commonly used when studying kundalini.

Aditya: Truth

Ahamkara: Egoism

Ahimsa: Nonviolence

Amrita: Eternal life

Asana: Posture, one of the five external limbs of yoga according to Patanjali

Astanga: Eight limbs of yoga described in Patanjali's Yoga Sutras

Atman: Self, Spirit, the soul, the deepest part of a person

Aum: Same as *Om*

Aura: Field outside of body

Avatara: Descent of a deity

Avidya: Ignorance, illusion, sometimes called maya

Bandhas: Exercises to release the bindings, or locks/granthis, to assist kundalini in rising

Bhagavad Gita: Song of the Blessed One, an important work to originate from India; part of the Mahabharata, written between 600 and 200 BC

Bhakti: Devotion, worship, love

Bodhi: Perfect knowledge or wisdom

Brahma: First of the triad of personalized gods (Brahma, Vishnu, Shiva); the Universal Spirit as Creator

Brahman: Godhead, Ultimate Reality, Vastness

Brahmin: One with the sacred knowledge

Buddha: Awakened, awake, enlightened; the proper name of the historical Siddhartha Gautama

Chakra: Center of energy connecting spiritual and physical self

Deva: God

Dharana: Focus, concentration; one of the eight limbs of Patanjali

Dharma: Law, order, obligation

Dharmashastra: Texts outlining requirements of dharma

Dhyana: Meditation, contemplation, one of the three internal limbs of yoga

Drstis: Gaze taking when doing a posture

Dukkha: Suffering

Elements: Five building blocks of the manifest world: earth, water, air, fire, space or ether

Granthi: Binding or locks affecting rise of kundalini

Gunas: Strand, constituent, the three gunas (satva, rajas, tamas) are the three fundamental components of the whole of prakriti, or nature

Guru: Teacher

Hatha: Force, joining of sun and moon

Ishvara: God, the Supreme Being

Kaivalya: Highest state of consciousness, according to Patanjali

Karma: Act, action, work; see *law of karma*

Klesas: Afflictions causing karma and suffering

Krishna: A teacher in the Bhagavad Gita, the eighth incarnation of Vishnu

Kriya: Action, work

Kundalini: Serpent energy (Shakti) that moves up the body between first and seventh chakras; when unified with crown chakra, one is unified with the Divine

Law of karma: Law of cause and effect applied to physical, moral, and psychological spheres, see *karma*

Linga: Mark, sign, trace; phallic symbol of Shiva

Locks: Bindings affecting the rise of kundalini (see *granthi*)

Manas: Lower mind, reason

Mandala: Circle

Mantra: Special sound given by a teacher as a discipline for recitation

Maya: Illusions, unreality, deception; Maya is illusion personified

Moksha: Unconditional freedom, liberation

Mudra: Hand gesture creating a specific energetic outcome

Mukti: Freedom, liberation, same as *moksha*

Muni: Sage

Nadis: Energy channels in body, affect path of kundalini

Nirvana: Extinction of selfish cravings

Niyama: Control, one of the five outer limbs of yoga

Om: Primordial vibration, most sacred syllable, same as *Aum*

Paramatma: The universal self

Prakriti: Nature, materiality, sometimes same as *maya*

Prana: Subtle energy, breath; same as *chi* in Chinese thought and *mana* in Polynesian

Pranayama: Regulation of prana, breath control, one of the five outer limbs of yoga

Pratyahara: Drawing back the senses, one of the five outer limbs of yoga

Prikrita: Natural, unrefined, vulgar

Purusha: Person, primal human, identified with Atman and Brahman

Raga: King

Rajas: The gunas or constituent of passion and activity

Ramayana: The great epic of Rama

Rig Veda: The oldest of the four Vedas and the oldest text in any Indo-European language; parts may date to 3000 BC

Rita: Cosmic order

Sadhaka: Aspirant, practitioner

Sadhana: Quest, effort

Samadhi: Joining, synthesis, integration, the eighth and last state of yoga

Samsara: Worldly life, secular, illusion; cycle of birth and death

Samskara: Impression

Samyama: Discipline, steady attention; last three limbs of yoga; control of mind

Sanatana: Eternal

Sanskrit: The sacred language of India

Santi: Peace, calm

Sanyasa: Renunciation

Sat-Karmas: Bodily cleaning techniques to purify body and mind

Satva: The guna of lucidity

Satya: Truth

Shakti: Energy, serpent power, the kundalini; feminine counterpoint of Shiva

Shiva: Lord of transformation, destruction, sleep; third of the Hindu triad of personalized gods (also including Brahma and Vishnu); the one who merges with Shakti

Siddhi: Power, attribute, gift

Soma: Yogic nectar, sacred juice

Sutra: A thread, a short rule or aphorism in the Sanskrit texts

Svabhava: Inner calling, essential nature

Svakarma: Karma relating to one's svabhava or essential self

Tamas: Inertia, sloth, stability; one of the three gunas

Tapas: Heat, austerity, penance, effort

Tapasya: Sustained practice and austerity

Upanishads: Sacred writings of the Hindus, the concluding portion of the Vedas, numbering over 200 works dating between 800 and 500 BC

Vasana: Innate tendency

Vayus: Winds of the body or components of breath

Veda: The most sacred literature of the Hindus; knowledge. There are four Vedas, the oldest (Rig Veda) composed around 1500 BC.

Vedanta: End of knowledge, end of the Veda; most influential school of philosophy in India

Vidya: Mental knowledge, wisdom

Vishnu: Second of the Hindu triad of gods, also including Brahma and Shiva; the preserver and sustainer

Yama: Lord of death and of dharma; yama is one of the five outer limbs of yoga

Yantra: Visual geometrical pattern

Yoga: Integration; union; the art of yoking; attaching; joining; meditation aiming at the union with Ishvara, or the Supreme Spirit; a path that creates that union

Yoga Sutra: One of the most important texts of yoga, attributed to Patanjali

Important Background Information

The Vedas

The Vedas are the original Sanskrit texts that form the foundation of Indian philosophy and yoga. They are written in poetic verse and have been chanted for generations, since at least 1500 BC. Some might date back to 3000 BC.

Rig Veda: First Veda, the source of mantra

Sama Veda: Second Veda, singing of mantras

Yajur Veda: Third Veda, application of mantras in ritual

Atharva Veda: Fourth Veda, supplementary mantras

Upanishads

These are the source of the Vedanta philosophy. The thirteen listed here are the most common. They are encapsulations of the Vedas and passed on orally by teacher to student.

Aitareya: Name of a sage

Brhad-Aranyaka: Great forest

Chandogya: Named after a part of the Veda

Isa: Lord

Katha: Named after a part of the Yajur Veda

Kausitaki: Name of sage who taught it

Kena: Discourse on Brahman, the Absolute Being

Maitri: Friendship

Mandukya: Name of sage who taught it

Mundaka: Shaved

Prasna: Question

Svetasvatara: White horse

Taittiriya: Named after a part of the Yajur Veda

Major Yoga Texts

Bhagavad Gita: Conversation between Krishna (God) and Arjuna (human); the divine song; part of the Mahabharata, which, along with the Ramayana, make up the two gigantic Indian epics

Gheranda Samhita: Treatise on hatha yoga

Hatha Yoga Pradipika: Treatise on hatha yoga, the illumination of Mahabharata: an epic story containing the Bhagavad Gita

Ramayana: Epic story about the life of Rama

Siva Samhita: Treatise on hatha yoga

Yoga-Darsana Yoga Sutras: by Patanjali

Yoga-Vasistha: Treatise on yoga

The Eight Limbs of Patanjali (Astanga)

1. Yama: Social restraints

2. Niyama: Personal ethics, internal restraints

3. Asana: Posture, sitting

4. Pranayama: Breath regulation

5. Pratyahara: Internalization of the senses, drawing back

6. Dharana: Focus, concentration

7. Dhyana: Maintaining a focus, meditation

8. Samadhi: Complete absorption

The Winds or Breaths (Vayus)

These are the *vayus*, or primary components of the breath, all governed by prana and affected by an asana.

Apana: Downward breath

Prana: Primary moving force, attention, primary breath

Samana: Equalizing breath

Vyana: Pervading breath

Udana: Upward breath

The Seven Primary Chakras

- First or base or root, coccyx, Muladhara
- Second, sacrum, Swadhisthana
- Third, solar plexus, Manipura
- Fourth, heart, Ahahata
- Fifth, throat, Vishuddha
- Sixth, brow or third eye, Ajna
- Seventh, crown, Sahasrara

1. www.answers.com/topic/kundalini and http://
   www.transpersonal.com.au/kundalini/definition
   .htm#definition.

2. Rice, *Eastern Definitions*, 231, and http://www
   .swamij.com/kundalini-awakening.htm.

3. Winternitz, *History of Indian Literature*, 587, and
   Bhattacharyya, *History of the Tantric Religion*, 20.

4. http://www.sivanandaonline.org/graphics/sadhana
   /YOGA/meaning.html.

5. http://www.hinduwebsite.com/tantra.asp.

6. Usha, *A Brief Dictionary of Hinduism*, 77, and
   White, *Tantra in Practice*, 7.

7. Birla, *Alive in Krishna: Living Memories of the Vedic
   Quest*, 37, and Radhakrishnan, *Indian Philosophy,
   Volume II*.

8. http://www.writespirit.net/inspirational_talks
   /spiritual/swami_vivekananda_talks/thoughts
   -on-women-swami-vivekananda/view.

9. http://www.writespirit.net/spirituality/kundalini
   /kundalini-vivekananda.

10. Shastri, *A Concise History of Classical Sanskrit Literature*, 5.

11. http://www.hinduwisdom.info/Sanskrit.htm.

12. www.answers.com/topic/kundalini and http://www.transpersonal.com.au/kundalini/definition.htm.

13. King, *Earth Energies: A Quest for the Hidden Power of the Planet*, ix–10.

14. http://www.swamij.com/kundalini-awakening-1.htm.

15. Dale, *The Subtle Body*, 273.

16. Ibid.

17. Ibid., 276.

18. www.kundalinicare.com/aboutkundalini3.html.

19. http://www.anmolmehta.com/blog/2008/01/03/kundalini-awakening-symptoms/ and http://www.kundalini-gateway.org/ksigns.html.

20. http://www.ahastories.com/spiritualemergen.html.

21. http://easternhealingarts.com/Articles/SpiritualEmergency.html and Grof, *Spiritual Emergency*.

22. Jack Kornfield, "Obstacles and Vicissitudes in Spiritual Practice," as quoted in *Spiritual Emergency* by Stanislov and Christina Grof, 140.

23. http://www.koausa.org/Kundalini/sex.html.

24. R. Narayan, A. Kamat, et. al. "Quantitative evaluation of muscle relaxation induced by kundalini yoga with the help of EMG integrator," *Indian J Physiol Pharmacol.* 1990 Oct; 34(4): 279–81.

25. E. L. Olivo, "Protection throughout the life span: the psycho-neuroimmunologic impact of Indo-Tibetan meditative and yogic practices." *Ann N Y Acad Sci.* 2009 Aug; 1172: 163–71.

26. S. B. Khalsa, G. S. Khalsa, et. al. "Evaluation of a residential Kundalini yoga lifestyle pilot program for addiction in India." *J Ethn Subst Abuse.* 2008; 7(1): 67–79.

27. D. S. Shannahoff-Khalsa, L. E. Ray, et. al. "Randomized controlled trial of yogic meditation techniques for patients with obsessive-compulsive disorder." *CNS Spectr.* 1999 Dec; 4(12): 34–47.

28. http://www.experiencefestival.com/a/Science_and _Spirituality/id/221200.

29. McTaggart, *The Field*, 43–55.

30. http://www.yogamag.net/archives/1979/joct79/kunref.shtml.

31. http://biologyofkundalini.com/article.php?story=Hormones.

32. http://biologyofkundalini.com/article.php?story= TheKundaliniGland.

33. McCraty, et al., *Science of the Heart*, 20.

34. Ibid.

35. http://www.miraclesandinspiration.com/pinealgland.html; http://tinyurl.com/2dwhn3p; http://tinyurl.com/2a2wota.

36. http://www.psi-researchcentre.co.uk/article_2.html.

37. A. Newberg, A. Alavi, et. al. "The measurement of regional cerebral blood flow during the complex cognitive task of meditation: a preliminary SPECT study." *Psychiatry Res.* 2001 Apr 10; 106(2): 113–22.

38. Peper, Arambula, and Gibney Kawakami, "The Physiological Correlates of Kundalini Yoga Meditation: A Study of a Yoga Master," *Appl Psychophysiol Biofeedback.* 2001 Jun; 26(2): 147–53.

39. www.whalemedical.com/nakedspirit/ns15.html.

40. J. C. Corby, W. T. Roth, et. al. "Psychophysiological correlates of the practice of Tantric Yoga meditation." *Arch Gen Psychiatry.* 1978 May; 35(5): 571–7.

41. www.whalemedical.com/nakedspirit/ns15.html.

42. http://www.kheper.net/topics/Tantra/history.htm.

43. Yogananda, *Autobiography of a Yogi*, 275.

44. http://www.kriya.org/about__kriya.php.

45. http://www.angelfire.com/yt/KRIYAYOGA/ministeng.html.

46. Johari, *Chakras: Energy Centers of Transformation*, 3.

47. Khalsa, *Kundalini Yoga*, 33.

48. http://hinduism.about.com/od/omaum/a/meaningofom
.htm and www.kundaliniyoga.org/mantra.html.

49. http://www.yogawiz.com/yoga-poses.html and http://www.
santosha.com/asanas/index-2.html.

50. Budilovsky and Adamson, revised with Carolyn Flynn, *The
Complete Idiot's Guide to Yoga*, 23–24, and http://www.ehow
.com/how_4975_mountain-pose-yoga.html.

51. http://chakraYoga.suite101.com.

52. Allison Lyke, "A Yoga for Each Chakra," http://chakrayoga
.suite101.com/article.cfm/a_yoga_for_each_chakra.

53. Khalsa, *Kundalini Yoga*, 30–31.

54. Ibid., 34–35.

55. Ibid., 87–102.

56. Ibid., 37–48.

57. Ibid., 41–44.

58. www.kundalini-teacher.com/initiations/shaktipat.php and
www.sacredspaceyogasanctuary.com/kunda2.html.

59. Farhi, *Yoga Mind, Body & Spirit*, 7–16.

60. http://www.clherbs.com/TECHNIQUES.htm.

61. http://www.tantra-kundalini.com/ and http://www.ehow
.com/how_2111539_push-lovers-boundaries-tantra.html.

62. http://eatdrinkbetter.com/2009/10/27/intentional
-chocolate-is-infused-with-love.

63. http://www.selfgrowth.com/articles/Feeding_the
_Chakras_7_Steps_to_Nourishing_Body_Mind_and_Soul
.html.

64. http://www.guardian.co.uk/lifeandstyle/2008/sep/23
/healthandwellbeing.pollution.

65. http://www.jenniferhawthorne.com/articles/change_your _thoughts.html.

66. http://www.sentientdevelopments.com/2007/03/managing -your-50000-daily-thoughts.html.

67. http://www.mayoclinic.com/health/positive-thinking /SR00009.

68. www.realiseyourinnerpotential.com/kundalini_article.html.

69. Bruyere, *Wheels of Light*, 84, and http://www.jeshua.net /healing/healing5.htm.

70. Jung, *The Psychology of Kundalini Yoga*, 22.

71. http://www.edgarcayce.org/ps2/kundalini_meditation _J_Van_Auken.html and www.heartnsoul.com/cayce _on_meditation.htm.

72. Field, *The Code of the Warrior*, 268.

73. www.kundaliniyoga.org/pranayam.html.

74. http://biologyofkundalini.com/article.php?story=Hormones.

75. Ibid.

76. kundaliniyoga.homestead.com/tantra.html.

77. Ibid.

78. http://www.iloveulove.com/spirituality/hindu/chakratantra .htm.

79. Khalsa, *Kundalini Yoga*, 34–35.

80. Ibid., 190–191.

81. www.scribd.com/doc/25053140/Salaat-The-Kundalini -Yoga-of-Islam.

82. www.transpersonal.com.au/divine-feminine.htm; www .sol.com.au/kor/14_02.htm; and www.womenutc.com /feminineimagesforgodinthebible1.htm.

83. Bruyere, *Wheels of Light*, 118–124.

84. Maheshwarananda, *The Hidden Power in Humans*, 47, 48, 49; www.siddhashram.org/kundalini.shtml; www.experience

festival.com/kundalini; Vivekananda, *The Complete Works of Swami Vivekananda*, 185.

85. http://samudra6.tripod.com/gkteeim.htm.

86. Ibid and Krishna, *Kundalini: The Evolutionary Energy in Man.*

87. http://www.experiencefestival.com/a/Gopi_Krishna /id/485530.

88. Ravindra, *The Spiritual Roots of Yoga*, 51.

89. Ibid., 4.

90. Ibid., 15.

91. Ibid., 15–17.

92. Wilber, *The Integral Vision*, 165.

93. http://www.authorsden.com/visit/viewPoetry.asp?id=63518.

Arambula, P., E. Peper, M. Kawakami, and K. H. Gibney. "The Physiological Correlates of Kundalini Yoga Meditation: A Study of a Yoga Master." *Applied Psychophysiology & Biofeedback* 26, no. 2 (June 2001): 147–53.

Arrindell, Willem A. "Masculine Gender Role Stress." *Psychiatric Times* (October 1, 2005).

Assagioli, Roberto. "Self-Realization and Psychological Disturbances," in *Spiritual Emergency*, edited by Stanislav Grof and Christina Grof. New York: Penguin/ Putnam, 1989.

Avalon, Arthur. *The Serpent Power*. New York: Dover Publications, 1964.

Bethards, Betty. *The Dream Book: Symbols for Self-Understanding*. Indianapolis: New Century Publishers, 2001.

Bhattacharyya, Narendra Nath. *History of the Tantric Religion*. New Delhi: Manohar, 1999.

bibliography

————. *The Indian Mother Goddess.* 3rd enl. ed. New Delhi: Manohar, 1999.

Birla, Ghanshyamdas. *Alive in Krishna: Living Memories of the Vedic Quest.* New York: Paragon House, 1986.

Blavatsky, H. P. *The Secret Doctrine.* Vol. 1. London: Theosophical University Press, 1888.

Bragdon, Emma. *A Sourcebook for Helping People in Spiritual Emergency.* San Francisco: Harper and Row, 1990.

————. *The Call of Spiritual Emergency: From Personal Crisis to Personal Transformation.* San Francisco: Harper and Row, 1990.

Brooks, Douglas Renfrew. *The Secret of the Three Cities: An Introduction to Hindu Sakta Tantrism.* Chicago: University of Chicago Press, 1990.

Bruyere, Rosalyn. *Wheels of Light.* Sierra Madre, CA: Bon Productions, 1989.

Budilovsky, Joan, and Eve Adamson; revised with Carolyn Flynn. *The Complete Idiot's Guide to Yoga.* New York: Penguin, 2006.

Burstin, Fay. "What's Killing Men." *Herald Sun* (Melbourne, Australia). October 15, 2005.

Canada, Geoffrey. "Learning to Fight." In *Men's Lives*, edited by Michael S. Kimmel and Michael A. Messner. Boston, London: Allyn and Bacon, 2001.

Caplan, Mariana. *Halfway Up the Mountain: The Error of Premature Claims to Enlightenment.* Prescott, AZ: Hohm Press, 1999.

Cavendish, Richard. *The Great Religions.* New York: Arco Publishing, 1980.

Cayce, Edgar. *The Lost Hall of Records.* Memphis, TN: Eagle Wings Books, 2000.

Chapman, J. "The Social Safety Net in Recovery from Psychosis: A Therapist's Story." *Psychiatric Services* 48 (1997): 461–462.

Chetanananda, S. *Dynamic Stillness.* Cambridge, MA: Rudra Press, 1991.

Cortright, Brant. *Psychotherapy and Spirit: Theory and Practice in Transpersonal Psychotherapy.* Albany, NY: State University of New York Press, 1997.

Courtenay, Will. "Constructions of Masculinity and Their Influence on Men's Well-Being: A Theory of Gender and Health." *Social Science and Medicine* 50, no. 10 (2000): 138–140.

Cromie, William J. "Research: Meditation Changes Temperatures: Mind Controls Body in Extreme Experiments." *Harvard University Gazette* (April 18, 2002).

Dale, Cyndi. *Advanced Chakra Healing.* Berkeley, CA: Crossings Press, 2005.

———. *The Subtle Body: An Encyclopedia of Your Energetic Anatomy.* Boulder, CO: Sounds True, 2009.

Farhi, Donna. *Yoga Mind, Body & Spirit.* New York: Henry Holt, 2000.

Field, Rick. *The Code of the Warrior.* New York: HarperPerennial, 1991.

Fisher, Helen. *The Anatomy of Love.* New York: Random House, 1992.

Frawley, David. *Yoga & Ayurveda: Self-Healing and Self-Realization.* Twin Lakes, WI: Lotus Press, 1999.

Gersten, Dennis. *Are You Getting Enlightened or Losing Your Mind? A Spiritual Program for Mental Fitness.* New York: Three Rivers Press/Harmony Books, 1997.

The Gheranda Samhita. Published with a commentary as *Pure Yoga* by Yogi Pranavananda, translated by Tony Rodriguez and Dr. Kanshi Ram. Delhi: Motilal Banarsidas, 1992.

Godwin, Joscelyn. *Mystery Religions in the Ancient World.* San Francisco, CA: Harper & Row, 1981.

The Gorakshashatakam. Critically edited and translated by Swami Kuvalayananda and Dr. S. A. Shukla. Kaivalyadhama, Lonavala (no date). A translation of a less critically edited edition is more readily available in chapter 14 of *Gorakhnath and the Kanphata Yogis* by George Weston Briggs (Delhi: Motilal Banarsidas, 1982).

Greenwell, Bonnie. *Energies of Transformation: A Guide to the Kundalini Process.* Cupertino, CA: Shakti River Press, 1990.

Greyson, Bruce. "Some Neuropsychological Correlates of the Physio-Kundalini Syndrome." *The Journal of Transpersonal Psychology* 32, no. 2 (2000).

Grof, Christina, and Stanislav Grof. *The Stormy Search for Self.* Los Angeles: Tarcher, 1990.

Grof, Stanislav, and Christina Grof, eds. *Spiritual Emergency: When Personal Transformation Becomes a Crisis.* Los Angeles: Tarcher, 1989.

Harper, Katherine Anne, and Robert L. Brown, eds. *The Roots of Tantra.* New York: State University of New York Press, 2002.

Harris, Barbara. *Spirtual Awakenings: A Guidebook for Experiencers and Those Who Care About Them.* Baltimore, MD: Stage 3 Books, 1993.

Harris, Barbara, and Lionel C. Bascom. *Full Circle: The Near-Death Experience and Beyond.* New York: Pocket Books, Simon and Schuster, 1990.

Hawley, John S., and Donna M. Wulff, eds. *Devi: Goddesses of India.* Berkeley: University of California Press, 1996.

Henderson, Joseph L., and Maud Oakes. *The Wisdom of the Serpent.* New Jersey: Princeton University Press, 1990.

———. *A History of Color.* Boston: Shambhala, 1991.

Hunt, Valerie V., Wayne W. Massey, Robert Weinberg, Rosalyn Bruyere, and Pierre M. Hahn. "A Study of Structural Integration from Neuromuscular, Energy Field, and Emotional Approaches." Sponsored by the Rolf Institute of Structural Integration, 1977; www.rolfing-craig-tracy.com /PDF/ucla.pdf.

Iyengar, B. K. S., and Yehudi Menuhin. *Light on Yoga: The Bible of Modern Yoga.* New York: Schocken, 1995.

Johari, Harish. *Chakras: Energy Centers of Transformation.* Rochester, VT: Destiny Books, 2000.

Jung, Carl. *The Psychology of Kundalini Yoga: Notes of the Seminar Given in 1932.* Lecture 1, 1 October 1932. Princeton, NJ: Princeton University Press, 1996.

Kason, Yvonne. *Farther Shores: Exploring How Near-Death, Kundalini and Mystical Experiences Can Transform Ordinary Lives.* Toronto: HarperCollins Publishers, 2000.

Katz, Richard. *Boiling Energy.* Cambridge: Harvard University Press, 1982.

Kaufman, Michael. "The Construction of Masculinity and the Triad of Men's Violence," in *Men's Lives,* edited by Michael S. Kimmel and Michael A. Messner. Boston, London: Allyn and Bacon, 2001.

Kennedy-Moore, Eileen, and Jeanne Watson. *Expressing Emotion.* New York: Guilford Press, 1999.

Khalsa, Gurmukh Kaur, and Cindy Crawford. *Bountiful, Beautiful, Blissful: Experience the Natural Power of Pregnancy.* New York: St. Martin's Press, 2003.

Khalsa, Gurmukh Kaur, Ken Wilber, and Swami Sivananda Radha. *Kundalini Rising: Exploring the Energy of Awakening.* Boulder, CO: Sounds True, 2009.

Khalsa, Shakta Kaur. *Kundalini Yoga.* New York: Dorley Kindersley Publishing, 2000.

King, Serge Kahili. *Earth Energies: A Quest for the Hidden Power of the Planet.* Wheaton, IL: Quest, 1992.

Kinsley, David R. *Hindu Goddesses: Visions of the Divine Feminine in the Hindu Religious Tradition.* Berkeley: University of California Press, 1986.

Kornfield, Jack. *A Path with Heart.* New York: Bantam Books, 1993.

———. "Obstacles and Vicissitudes in Spiritual Practice," in *Spiritual Emergency: When Personal Transformation Becomes A Crisis,* edited by Stanislav Grof and Christina Grof. Los Angeles: Tarcher, 1989.

Krishna, Gopi. *Kundalini: The Evolutionary Energy in Man.* London: Stuart & Watkins, 1970.

———. *Living with Kundalini.* Boulder, CO: Shambhala, 1993.

Lazar, Sara W., George Bush, Randy L. Gollub, Gregory L. Fricchione, Gurucharan Khalsa, Herbert Benson. "Functional Brain Mapping of the Relaxation Response and Meditation." *NeuroReport* 11, no. 7 (May 15, 2000): 1581–1585.

Louchakova, Olga. "Kundalini and Health," in *Kundalini Rising,* by Gurmukh Kaur Khalsa, Ken Wilber, and Swami Sivananda Radha. Boulder, CO: Sounds True, 2009.

Lukoff, D. "The Diagnosis of Mystical Experiences with Psychotic Features." *Journal of Transpersonal Psychology* 17 (1985): 155–181.

———. "Emergence of a Contemporary Shaman: A Case Study of Possession in the Dojo." Ninth International Conference on Shamanism, 1992.

———. "Transpersonal Therapy with a Manic-Depressive Artist." *Journal of Transpersonal Psychology* 20, no. 1 (1988): 10–20.

———. "Visionary Spiritual Experience." *Southern Medical Journal* 100, no. 6 (June 2007).

Lukoff, D., and F. Lu. "Cultural Competence Includes Religious and Spiritual Issues in Clinical Practice." *Psychiatric Annals* 29, no. 8 (1999): 469–472.

Lukoff, D., F. Lu, and R. Turner. "Commentary on 'Spiritual Experience and Psychopathology.'" *Philosophy, Psychiatry & Psychology* 4, no. 1 (March 1997).

———. "From Spiritual Emergency to Spiritual Problem: The Transpersonal Roots of the New DSM-IV Category." *Journal of Humanistic Psychology* 38, no. 2 (1998): 21–50.

Maheshwarananda, Paramhans Swami. *The Hidden Power in Humans: Chakras and Kundalini.* Vienna: Ibera Verlag, 2004.

Maslow, Abraham H. *Religions, Values, and Peak-Experiences.* New York: Viking Penguin, 1970.

———. *Toward a Psychology of Being.* New York: D. Van Nostrand Company, Inc., 1962.

McCraty, Rollin, Mike Atkinson, and Dana Tomasina, compilers. *Science of the Heart.* Publication No. 01-001. Boulder Creek, CA: HeartMath Institute, 2001.

McTaggart, Lynne. *The Field.* New York: Harper Perennial, 2003.

Melchizedek, Drunvalo. *Serpent of Light.* San Franscisco: Red Wheel/Weiser: 2008.

Men, Hunbatz. *Secrets of Mayan Science/Religion.* Rochester, VT: Bear & Co., 1989.

Minich, Deanna. *Chakra Foods for Optimum Health.* San Francisco, CA: Red Wheel/Weiser, 2009.

Moody, Raymond A. *Life After Life: The Investigation of a Phenomenon—Survival of Bodily Death.* New York: Bantam, 1975.

Morse, Melvin, with Paul Perry. *Closer to the Light.* New York: Ivy Books, 1990.

————. *Transformed by the Light: The Powerful Effect of Near-Death Experiences on People's Lives*. New York: Villard Books, 1992.

Muktananda, Swami. *From the Finite to the Infinite*. 1st ed., volumes I & II. South Fallsburg, NY: Siddha Yoga Dham of America Foundation, 1989.

Myss, Caroline. *Spiritual Madness: The Necessity of Meeting God in Darkness*. Audiobook; unabridged edition. Boulder, CO: Sounds True, 2002.

Narayan, R., A. Kamat, M. Khanolkar, S. Kamat, S. R. Desai, and R. A. Dhume. "Quantitative Evaluation of Muscle Relaxation Induced by Kundalini Yoga with the Help of EMG Integrator." *Indian J Physiol Pharmacol* 34, no. 4 (October 1990): 279–281.

Peng, C. K., J. E. Mietus, Y. Liu, G. Khalsa, P. S. Douglas, H. Benson, and A. L. Goldberger. "Exaggerated Heart Rate Oscillations During Two Meditation Techniques." *Int J Cardiol* 70, no. 2 (July 31, 1999): 101–107.

Pinkham, Mark Amaru. *The Return of the Serpents of Wisdom*. Kempton, IL: Adventures Unlimited Press, 1997.

Pintchman, Tracy. *The Rise of the Goddess in the Hindu Tradition*. Albany, NY: State University of New York Press, 1994.

Radhakrishnan, S. *Indian Philosophy*. Volume II. London: Oxford University Press, 1997.

Ravindra, Ravi. *The Spiritual Roots of Yoga*. Sandpoint, ID: Morning Light Press, 2006.

Rice, Edward. *Eastern Definitions*. New York: Doubleday, 1980.

Ring, Kenneth. *Heading Toward Omega: In Search of the Meaning of Near-Death Experiences*. New York: William Morrow, 1984.

————. *The Omega Project*. New York: William Morrow, 1992.

Sannella, Lee. *The Kundalini Experience*. Lower Lake, CA: Integral Publishing, 1992.

———. *Kundalini: Psychosis or Transcendence?* San Francisco: H. S. Dakin, 1976.

Saraswati, H. D. *Swami Prakashanand: The True History and the Religion of India*. Jagadguru Kripalu Parishat, Barsana Dham, 2003.

Scotton, Bruce W., Allan B. Chinen, and John R. Battista, editors. *The Phenomenology and Treatment of Kundalini*. New York: Basic Books, 1996.

———, editors. *Textbook of Transpersonal Psychiatry and Psychology*. New York: Basic Books, 1996.

Shannahoff-Khalsa, D. *Kundalini Yoga Meditation: Techniques Specific for Psychiatric Disorders, Couples Therapy, and Personal Growth*. New York: W. W. Norton & Company, 2006.

———. "An Introduction to Kundalini Yoga Meditation Techniques That are Specific for the Treatment of Psychiatric Disorders." *The Journal of Alternative and Complementary Medicine* 10, no. 1 (2004): 91–101.

Shastri, Gaurinath Bhattacharyya. *A Concise History of Classical Sanskrit Literature*. 2nd revised edition. Delhi: Motilala Banarsidas Publishers, 1960.

The Shiva Samhita. Translated by Rai Bahadur Srisa Chandra Vasu. Delhi: Sri Satguru, 1979.

Sivananda, Sri Swami. "Conquest of Anger." The Divine Life Society, World Wide Web Edition: 1999, http://www.dlshq.org/download/anger.pdf.

Small, Jacquelyn. *Transformers: The Artists of Self-Creation*. Camarillo, CA: DeVorss & Company, 1994.

Sovatsky, Stuart. *Words from the Soul: Time, East/West Spirituality, and Psychotherapeutic Narrative*. Suny Series in

Transpersonal and Humanistic Psychology. New York: State University of New York Press, 1998.

Stein, Diane. *Healing with Gemstones and Crystals.* Berkeley: Crossings Press, 1996.

———. *The Women's Book of Healing.* Berkeley, CA: Crossings Press, 1986.

Stone, Merlin. *When God Was a Woman.* New York: Harcourt Brace Jovanovich, 1976.

Svatmarama. *The Hatha Yoga Pradipika.* Translated with a commentary by Swami Muktibodhananda (a disciple of Swami Satyananda Saraswati). Bihar: Bihar School of Yoga, 1985.

Tirtha, Swami Vishnu. *Devatma Shakti.* Fifth ed. Rishikesh: Yoga Shri Peeth Trust, 1980.

Usha, Brahmacharini. *A Brief Dictionary of Hinduism.* Hollywood, CA: Vedanta Press, 1990.

Venkatesh S., T. R. Raju, Y. Shivani, G. Tompkins, and B. L. Meti. "A Study of Structure of Phenomenology of Consciousness in Meditative and Non-Meditative States." *Indian J Physiol Pharmacol* 41, no. 2 (April 1997): 149–153.

Vivekananda, Swami. *The Complete Works of Swami Vivekananda.* London, New York: Longmans, Green, and Co., 1915.

Walters, Dorothy. "Kundalini and the Mystic Path," in *Kundalini Rising* by Gurmukh Kaur Khalsa, Ken Wilber, and Swami Sivananda Radha. Boulder, CO: Sounds True, 2009.

Warrington, Freda. *Elfland.* New York: Tor Books/Tom Doherty Associates, 2009.

Waters, Frank. *Book of the Hopi.* New York: Ballantine Books, 1963.

White, David Gordon, ed. *Tantra in Practice.* Princeton, NJ: Princeton University Press, 2000.

White, John, editor. *Kundalini: Evolution and Enlightenment.* New York: Paragon House, 1990.

Whitfield, Barbara Harris. *Spiritual Awakenings: Insights of the Near-Death Experience and Other Doorways to Our Soul.* Deerfield Beach, FL: Health Communications, Inc., 1995.

Wilber, Ken. *The Integral Vision.* Boston: Shambhala, 2007.

Wills-Brandon, Carla. *A Glimpse of Heaven: The Remarkable World of Spiritually Transformative Experiences.* Avon, MA: Adams Media, 2004.

Winternitz, Maurice. *History of Indian Literature.* Volume I. New Delhi: Oriental Books Reprint Corporation, 1972.

Woodroffe, John George. *Sakti and Sakta: Essays and Addresses.* Eighth ed. Madras: Ganesh, 1975.

Yogananda, Paramahansa. *Autobiography of a Yogi.* Twelfth ed. Los Angeles: Self-Realization Fellowship, 1993.

Ywahoo, Dhyani. *Voices of Our Ancestors.* Boston: Shambhala, 1987.

GET MORE AT LLEWELLYN.COM

Visit us online to browse hundreds of our books and decks, plus sign up to receive our e-newsletters and exclusive online offers.

- **Free tarot readings • Spell-a-Day • Moon phases**
- **Recipes, spells, and tips • Blogs • Encyclopedia**
- **Author interviews, articles, and upcoming events**

GET SOCIAL WITH LLEWELLYN

Find us on Facebook

www.Facebook.com/LlewellynBooks

Follow us on

www.Twitter.com/Llewellynbooks

GET BOOKS AT LLEWELLYN

LLEWELLYN ORDERING INFORMATION

 Order online: Visit our website at www.llewellyn.com to select your books and place an order on our secure server.

 Order by phone:
- Call toll free within the U.S. at 1-877-NEW-WRLD (1-877-639-9753)
- Call toll free within Canada at 1-866-NEW-WRLD (1-866-639-9753)
- We accept VISA, MasterCard, and American Express

 Order by mail:
Send the full price of your order (MN residents add 6.875% sales tax) in U.S. funds, plus postage and handling to: Llewellyn Worldwide, 2143 Wooddale Drive, Woodbury, MN 55125-2989

POSTAGE AND HANDLING
STANDARD (U.S. & Canada):
(Please allow 12 business days)
$25.00 and under, add $4.00.
$25.01 and over, FREE SHIPPING.

INTERNATIONAL ORDERS (airmail only):
$16.00 for one book, plus $3.00 for each additional book.

Visit us online for more shipping options.

Prices subject to change.

FREE CATALOG!

To order, call
1-877-
NEW-WRLD
ext. 8236
or visit our
website

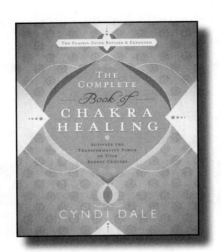

The Complete Book of Chakra Healing
Activate the Transformative Power of Your Energy Centers

Cyndi Dale

When first published in 1996 (as *New Chakra Healing*), Cyndi Dale's guide to the chakras established a new standard for healers, intuitives, and energy workers worldwide. This groundbreaking book quickly became a bestseller. It expanded the seven-chakra system to thirty-two chakras, explained spiritual points available for dynamic change, and outlined the energetic system so anyone could use it for health, prosperity, and happiness.

Presented here for the first time is the updated and expanded edition, now titled *The Complete Book of Chakra Healing*. With nearly 150 more pages than the original book, this groundbreaking edition is poised to become the next classic guide to the chakras. This volume presents a wealth of valuable new material:

- The latest scientific research explaining the subtle energy system and how it creates the physical world
- Depiction of the negative influences that cause disease, as well as ways to deal with them
- Explanations of two dozen energy bodies plus the meridians and their uses for healing and manifesting

978-0-7387-1502-5 • 7½ x 9⅛, 456 pp. • illus., charts, bibliog., index • $24.95

To order, call 1-877-NEW-WRLD
Prices subject to change without notice
Order at Llewellyn.com 24 hours a day, 7 days a week!

Extraordinary Answers to Finding Love,
Destiny and Balance in Your Life

Everyday Clairvoyant

Cyndi Dale

Everyday Clairvoyant
*Extraordinary Answers to Finding Love,
Destiny and Balance in Your Life*

Cyndi Dale

This engaging book from professional clairvoyant and best-selling author Cyndi Dale features true personal stories and practical advice on how to handle everything from everyday concerns to major life decisions. Cyndi has provided intuitive consulting and healing to more than thirty thousand individuals, helping them lead more successful, happy, and prosperous lives. In this fascinating book, she shares what she's learned with readers in a fun Q & A format that is organized into three categories: relationships, work or destiny, and health. Heartwarming, humorous, and surprisingly down to earth, *Everyday Clairvoyant* also shows readers how to develop and make use of their own intuitive gifts.

978-0-7387-1923-8 • 5³⁄₁₆ x 8, 312 pp.
• charts, appendices • $16.95

To Write to the Author

If you wish to contact the author or would like more information about this book, please write to the author in care of Llewellyn Worldwide and we will forward your request. Both the author and the publisher appreciate hearing from you and learning of your enjoyment of this book and how it has helped you. Llewellyn Worldwide cannot guarantee that every letter written to the author can be answered, but all will be forwarded. Please write to:

Cyndi Dale
c/o Llewellyn Worldwide
2143 Wooddale Drive
Woodbury, MN 55125-2989

Please enclose a self-addressed stamped envelope for reply,
or $1.00 to cover costs. If outside U.S.A., enclose
international postal reply coupon.

Many of Llewellyn's authors have websites with additional information and resources. For more information, please visit our website:

http://www.llewellyn.com